How to get FITTER . . . *faster*

The no-nonsense guide to fast-tracking YOUR health & fitness

Mike Searle

Congratulations on completing the Extra Mile Challenge!

Best Wishes,

Mike Searle

SLC Press

How to get FITTER **. . . *faster***

www.body4life.co.uk

A catalogue record for this book is available from the British Library

ISBN 978-0-9557834-0-1

First Published in Great Britain in 2008

by

SLC Press

Printed and bound in Great Britain for SLC Press

The publisher's policy is to use paper manufactured from sustainable forests

How to get FITTER . . . *faster*

To Cath,

for your enduring support

Contents

Introduction

> *'He who has health has hope and he who has hope has everything'.*
>
> **ARABIAN PROVERB**

With the ever increasing pace and pressures of 21st century living showing no signs of abating, how do you manage to accommodate health and fitness issues into your life? The likely answer is *'with difficulty'* because so many people nowadays are struggling with:

- Weight management issues
- Finding sufficient time for exercise
- Knowing exactly what, when and how they should be exercising

If any of those scenarios sound all too familiar to you with our *'I want it yesterday culture'* and the continual pressures of telephone, e-mail and deadlines then read on.

Finding time for your personal health and fitness can be challenging to say the least but in our increasingly labour-saving and sedentary world, your health and fitness has never been more important. Our modern lives are extremely different to only a few years ago and a great many of the current ills that people are suffering from such as weight management problems and many preventable diseases, are a direct result of lifestyle changes in activity levels and nutrition.

How to get fitter . . . *faster* has been specifically written with these problems in mind, focusing upon everything that you need to get fit, stay fit and reap the massive benefits of following a healthy lifestyle.

If you would like:

- Good health
- More energy
- Better posture
- Better quality sleep
- A positive body image
- Greater self-confidence
- Easier weight management
- A reduced risk of preventable diseases

together with the knowledge and motivation to achieve your personal health and fitness goals then this is the book for you.

Written by Mike Searle, the UK's leading, motivational and innovative Personal Trainer, **How to get fitter . . . *faster*** will inspire, educate and motivate you to improve your health and fitness, just as Mike has achieved with body4life, his groundbreaking and successful Personal Training Company. (**www.body4life.co.uk**). With body4life, Mike has set unrivalled standards of excellence for Personal Training and helped countless people improve the quality of their lives and 'get fitter . . . faster'.

Mike's straight-talking, no-nonsense style of writing has earned him numerous plaudits and **How to get fitter . . . *faster*** is a refreshingly honest, accurate and readable health and fitness manual, combined with a dash of humour, which will help you get fitter . . . faster.

Author's note

How to get fitter . . . *faster* is not a ghost-written book with my name on the front. I have personally written every single word on every single page and in every single chapter, which is a process that I have enjoyed immensely. Distilling years of practical experience from my own training and competition successes, together with thousands and thousands of one-to-one personal training sessions training people of all ages and fitness levels, has provided me with a wealth of material to draw upon in creating this volume. Helping so many people to not only achieve their goals but to exceed them and achieve far more than they ever dreamed was possible has been incredibly rewarding and writing this book has given me the opportunity to share my tips, secrets and techniques with a wider audience. I hope that you enjoy reading this work and I am certain that you will find it a constant source of practical help and motivation that you will return to again and again.

Enjoy your training.

www.body4life.co.uk

The benefits of using this book

There are a multitude of fitness books available which picture exercise after exercise in a textbook - but that doesn't help you much when you're actually at the gym or exercising. Firstly, it's totally impractical to carry a book around with you during your workout and secondly, if you're looking to get the best out of your training then far more critical factors are the structure and the specific components of your training programme, which are the foundations of your success.

You are unique and hence your exercise programme should also be unique to you. Your exercise schedule should factor in your age, sex, current fitness levels, goals and any pre-conditions which you may have because a 'one-size-fits-all' approach not only won't work, it's positively dangerous. For example, take a walk down your local High Street and you won't see many 'one-size-fits-all' people. Safety and technique are equally of paramount importance.

Hence, **How to get fitter . . . *faster*** is different. This book focuses on all the components of a balanced fitness programme, neatly categorised into separate chapters covering a broad spectrum of health and fitness issues that serves as an ideal reference book for every element of your fitness. **How to get fitter . . . *faster*** is packed with ideas, suggestions and my proven exercise strategies and tips that I have personally tried, tested, revised and perfected, covering all aspects of the optimum way to exercise and improve your health and fitness.

How to get fitter . . . *faster* is deliberately structured in an A-Z format that facilitates easy reading, with short, punchy chapters written in a no-nonsense style and packed with tips that really work. Simply dip in to any chapter, in any order and you are guaranteed to find tips and advice to help you get more out of your health and fitness programme.

Safety first

Regular exercise is imperative for your health and embarking on a structured exercise programme can only improve your short and long-term fitness. However, before you begin, your first step should be to honestly assess your current fitness levels. First, complete the Health Status Questionnaire below to ensure that you do not risk injury or something more serious.

If you answer **YES** to one or more questions, book an appointment with your GP to discuss your exercise plans. Your Doctor will certainly welcome your plans to improve your fitness and will also be able to advise you if there are any specific precautions that you should take relevant to your personal medical history.

If you answer all '**NO's**' to the questionnaire and / or your Doctor gives you the 'all-clear' then you're ready to start improving your health and fitness.

Health Status Questionnaire

Complete the questionnaire by answering each question honestly and accurately, based on your current lifestyle and levels of fitness, rather than historical fitness levels. If you are in any doubt then consult your Doctor.

1. Are you aged over 30?
2. Are you a smoker or have you recently given up smoking?
3. Have you undergone any major surgery in the past ten years or any minor surgery in the past two years?
4. Are you currently on any prescribed medication?
5. Do you suffer from any medical conditions?
6. Are you pregnant or have you given birth in the last 12 months?
7. Was your most recent, <u>regular</u> exercise over 12 months ago?
8. Do you have any areas of soreness around the body?
9. Are you suffering from any known injuries?
10. Do you suffer from any other health conditions?
11. Are you at all unsure about beginning an exercise programme?
12. Is your Body Mass Index above 25?

    (See the following example to check your Body Mass Index)

QuickTest

How to calculate your Body Mass Index (BMI)

BMI is a rule of thumb guide to body composition, giving an approximate indication whether an adult is within the recommended weight limits for their height. The desirable range for adult men and women is a BMI reading from 20-25

To check your BMI

1. ***You need to know your weight (in Kg) and your height (in metres).***

2. ***Take your weight and divide it by your height squared.***

Eg: To calculate the BMI for a 70Kg person who is 1.7 metres tall:

$$BMI = \frac{\text{Weight in Kg}}{\text{Height in metres}^2} = \frac{70}{1.7 \times 1.7} = \frac{70}{2.89} = 24.22$$

This person is within the recommended BMI limits of 20-25

Aging

> *'Most of the decline that comes with old age isn't inevitable at all. It's caused by disuse'.* **DR KENNETH COOPER**

Exercise for LIFE!

Many people believe that a decline in health and fitness is an inevitable part of the aging process and view aches, pains, weaker muscles and the inability to carry out everyday tasks as *'c'est la vie'.* Well I fervently disagree. A great many of these 'old age problems' are not the direct result of ageing, but due to the lack of physical activity that often occurs as we get older. I believe that it is time to challenge these misconceptions because there is considerable evidence that age-related decline can be avoided and even reversed, providing that you continue to exercise.

There are numerous examples of elite sportspeople who despite their age have still competed at the very highest level and we don't have to accept that when we hit 30, 40, 50 or even pension-able age, that all is lost because it certainly isn't. You don't need to be an elite athlete to achieve and reap the rewards so let's start by looking at the Top 5 benefits from exercising as you get older.

Top 5 exercise benefits as you age

1. **Increased strength.** Between the ages of 30 and 80, as much as 60% of your muscular strength can be lost – unless you take remedial action. By following an all-over body training programme twice a week, you can not only prevent strength losses but can actually reverse the process. Be careful to follow correct training protocols when working out with weights so that you can tone up, firm up and straighten up safely.

2. **Improved aerobic capacity.** Puffed out walking up hills? Combined with the ageing process, sedentary lifestyles contribute to lower cardiovascular capability. However, as little as three brisk walks of 20 minutes each week will go a long way to halting the decline, so that those hills now seem pretty flat!

3. **A strong skeleton.** Statistics show that osteoporosis, or brittle bone disease, currently affects 50% of women and 20% of men over the age of 50, which is a huge total. Impact activities such as walking and jogging, combined with resistance training (which will strengthen the upper skeleton), will offset this debilitating disease.

4. **Easy weight management.** In tandem with lower levels of activity often comes weight gain, which then becomes harder to shift because of lower levels of activity – and so on. However, by getting involved in a correctly prescribed exercise programme, it becomes much easier to balance the calories against your activity levels, making it easier to keep your weight in check.

5. **Greater brain power!** Yes it's true. Studies in America on two groups of people, one of whom was on a mild aerobic exercise programme, whilst the other did no cardiovascular exercise, resulted in the exercise group achieving an 11% improvement in mental tests. Increased blood flow to the brain, combined with the release of chemicals which influence the growth of brain cells is thought to be responsible for the improvement.

So, an impressive package of benefits - what a great incentive to get fit and stay fit, whatever your age!

Exercise through the years!

Old Father Time is bearing down upon us all but does that mean that once the first flush of youth has passed we're all designated for the scrap heap? I don't think so! What is key, is to focus upon maintaining fitness throughout our lives and indeed as we get older, that becomes increasingly more important. Numerous studies have shown that maintaining activity levels and specific training to improve flexibility, strength and aerobic fitness not only helps keep the Grim Reaper at bay but can actually reverse the decline that is frequently perceived as inevitable as we get older. Whilst replicating physical feats achieved in our youth may no longer be achievable; keeping supple, strong and being able to keep up with the kids certainly is!

So let's look at specific strategies that you can employ in the battle of advancing years, so that you can improve the quality of your life as you get older.

Top tips to maintain fitness down the decades

- **Before you're 20.** Have fun. Try different sports, different activities and different sorts of exercise so that you get all round physical development and you're also able to identify the activities that you prefer. Try not to focus all your attention on a sole sport because not only may you miss out on other exciting activities, you also run the risk of developing imbalances because your body is still growing. For example, don't simply go to the gym to lift weights, neglecting aerobic training.

- **In your 20's.** Physically, you're at your peak, enjoying faster recovery, more speed and a deep well of energy, so this decade is the time to develop good exercise habits. Ensure that you're building the habit of exercising regularly, so that it's a part of your life, which you can then carry forward into your later years. Focus on learning correct technique now because it is much harder to 'unlearn' poor technique once it has become ingrained. Make sure that you don't neglect aerobic training because it can take many years to really build stamina, so start now so that you have a good foundation.

- **In your 30's.** Build strength. Nature dictates that without any conditioning training, from hereon in, you will start to lose muscle mass. Hence this decade is key for building muscle so that you can counteract the wastage that can occur with age. Thereafter you can focus upon maintaining your strength during later years. Look to work out in the gym twice a week and try to gradually challenge your body to lift heavier weights, always focusing upon perfect technique.

- **In your 40's**. This is a danger period for anyone active in exercise. Again and again I see people suffering from soft tissue injuries once they hit 40, yet the majority of these injuries are preventable. Muscle pulls and strains become much more common as age related dehydration and lifestyle related flexibility problems take hold, so you need to focus upon adding additional flexibility training into your routine. Spend time stretching out all the major muscle groups of the body twice a week.

- **In your 50's.** A bit of everything. Whatever your age you need to keep your exercise programme balanced, covering all the disciplines of strength, co-ordination, flexibility and aerobic fitness and by now you should have developed good training habits so this decade is the one to maintain a little bit of everything.

- **In your 60's.** Recovery is key. As you get older, you will find that your recovery from an exercise session takes longer and you generally need more rest. Hence in your 60's, seek to maintain the same volume and intensity of the training that you followed in earlier years but allow yourself longer rest periods and an extra day off. For example, the runner who raced on a Sunday and could then knock out a quality interval session the next Tuesday will find that they'll probably need an extra day or so to allow their body sufficient time to recover. This way you can still maintain a high level of fitness and also avoid injury.

- **In your 70's.** Well done! When you reach your 70's, set your own pace. By know you will have a good feel for what you can and can't achieve and your own limits, so listen to your body and react accordingly. If you feel that you need to curtail a session or take an extra rest day – just do it because your primary focus is maintenance, enjoyment and enhancing the quality of your life.

- **Beyond your 70's.** It's never too late. Whatever your age, exercising will have a beneficial effect on your body, your state of mind and of course your quality of life so whatever forms of exercise you enjoy; keep it going. The fitter you have been pre age 70, the fitter you will be now, which cements the importance of building your fitness routine right from your 20's and then carrying it through as you get older.

Exercise – the elixir of youth!

The search for the elixir of youth could be much closer than we think! Yes, it's absolutely true because research has found that the typical gradual decline in muscle strength, muscle mass and muscle functionality that is expected with age can be reversed. A Canadian study focused on a group of pensioners, each with an average age of 70, who followed a carefully structured training programme of resistance training exercises over a period of six months. Prior to the programme, the pensioners' strength had declined to a level such that on average they were 59% weaker than a sample group of adults aged 20-35 years. However after their training, they were only 38% weaker – a massive improvement of almost 50%! At a more physiological level, the scientists found that the changes within the cells that are associated with aging, reversed back to levels that would be expected with much younger adults. Effectively, this demonstrates that regular exercise can keep you younger – for longer - and everyone can buy into that concept.

So, what does the older exerciser need to do to get similar gains and remain strong right into old age? Simply follow the top anti-aging fitness tips below to reap similar benefits.

How to build strength when you're older

1. **Get assessed.** This is important for anyone who is embarking upon a strengthening fitness programme but absolutely imperative for an older person, to be comprehensively assessed prior to starting to exercise. Age related muscle imbalances, flexibility and postural problems, combined with the increased possibility of prior medical conditions means that if you are not assessed then you risk injury or further complications. Following assessment, your

training can be correctly structured for you, your needs and your fitness levels, which will result in faster progression.

2. **Small gains mean consistent gains.** When you're older, naturally you will take longer to recover from a workout and your body will also take longer to reap the rewards of your exercise sessions. So look for small and regular improvements, rather than quantum leaps forward in your fitness levels and you will gradually and safely get fitter and stronger.

3. **Start slowly.** To begin with, you need to become familiar with the equipment, the environment and gradually allow your body to come to terms with the new demands that you'll be making upon it. Don't think that this is wasted time, far from it, it is extremely important to introduce your body to correct training protocols at a sensible pace. Give yourself time and enjoy the introductory phase.

4. **Technique is everything!** The initial familiarisation period is the optimum time to learn correct technique – not only for the movements associated with each exercise but for the other movements and positional techniques that you need to learn for exercising safely. Use only light weights and don't risk progressing further until you can execute each movement perfectly – or otherwise you could risk injury.

5. **Take a break!** When working out with weights, it is common to perform two or more sets of an exercise, separated by a recovery period but when you are older, you may need to take a longer recovery before repeating an exercise. The key here is to react to how you're feeling and work at your own, personal level and pace, not that of anyone else. Everyone is different, so remember that it's about you, your workout, your goals and your session – not a competition with anyone else.

6. **Take a longer break!** After your weights workout, you will need to allow time for your body to adapt to the new training demands before you train again. Now for a younger person, they could be exercising on successive days but when you're older, it's likely that you will need more recovery. Hence, look for a minimum of two days between your exercise sessions; take longer if you feel you need it.

7. **Extra stretching!** Muscles lose elasticity with age but a programme of regular stretching will go a long way to reversing the age related decline in flexibility that is very prevalent amongst older

people. Hence as part of your training programme, you need to devote more time to stretching than a younger person, focusing upon not only the specific muscles that you have exercised during your session but the whole body, so that you remain supple, mobile and injury free.

8. **Don't get comfortable!** We all have particular exercises that we favour or prefer – usually because we're better at them. However, if you do the same exercises, the same way, every time then you will rapidly plateau with your training – which is very de-motivating. When you're older, you may be uncomfortable in stepping outside your comfort zone with your workout but believe me, providing you have professional instruction to ensure safety and suitability, you will get fitter faster if you include plenty of variety in your workouts.

Back Care

> *'Back pain is pandemic. It permeates all nationalities, all social groups and all professions and is second only to the common cold as a cause of time off work'.*
> ***SARAH KEY, BACK SPECIALIST***

Watch your back!

The back is a problem area for many people because it is an area of the body that is often neglected – often with disastrous consequences. Whether you are training in the gym or just lifting an object at home, lifting with correct technique is absolutely imperative to avoid injury.

Let's consider how you usually pick up an object from the floor:

1. Do you lean forward from the hips, rounding your spine towards the floor until you can reach the object with your hand?

2. Alternatively, keeping your body upright, do you bend at the knees and squat down until you can reach the object, using the large strong muscles of the thighs to control your movement?

If you answered (1) to the question above, you're like the vast majority of people, who *'save their legs'* and use their back to take the strain. And taking the strain is exactly what your back does with that bending movement. By rounding the spine as you lean forward, you place tremendous stress upon your lower back which can easily lead to the common condition known as a 'slipped disc'.

The correct way to retrieve an object from the floor is (2), which ensures that this most important region of your body is not subjected to unnecessary and potentially damaging loading.

Your back is a very complex structure, composed of 33 bones which are surrounded and supported by over 400 muscles. Your spine and back should be like a strong, flexible cable but it is often the weak link in the body due to one or more of the following conditions: poor posture, general back muscle weakness, undeveloped abdominal muscles, insufficient core strength, muscle imbalances, incorrect lifting technique and lifestyle problems.

To help prevent back problems, follow these back saving tips to strengthen this important area.

Back saving tips

1. **Walk Tall.** Poor posture is a key contributor to back pain, imbalances and weakness because it has a continual effect throughout the day. Whether you are walking, sitting or moving in any way, all the time that you are awake, you can help strengthen your back. Focus on walking upright with your shoulders back, stomach held in and head erect, avoid slouching across a desk or on a sofa at home and when standing, avoid distributing your weight onto one hip which initiates curvature of the spine. Instead, stand with both feet flat on the floor, legs straight, completely upright.

SuperTip

To help you focus on maintaining good posture, imagine that there's a hook attached to the top of your head, pulling you upwards towards the ceiling whenever you walk. Think of walking with a tall, relaxed posture instead of being hunched over.

2. **Ignore the mirror!** It is common when exercising to train the muscle groups that can be seen in the mirror. Looking at the upper body, the favourites are the chest and stomach. However, if the opposing muscle groups, (ie: their counterparts in your back) are ignored, imbalances and weaknesses can occur. Hence, it is important to exercise the lower and upper back at just the same intensity.

3. **Sit-up, sit-up!** Every woman who has had a baby will tell you that in the latter stages of pregnancy, they suffered from back pain. The reason for this is because the growing baby stretches and weakens the mother's abdominal muscles, resulting in excessive curvature of the lower spine and considerable back discomfort. If your stomach muscles are at all weak, then on a smaller scale, you are replicating the problems that a mother experiences when pregnant, resulting in lower back pain. By keeping your stomach muscles well toned, you help negate this effect.

4. **Work your core.** Your core muscles are deep postural muscles that run right around your abdomen, rather like a corset. They hold you in, help keep you upright and provide all-round back strength and training your core muscles is absolutely key to building your back.

5. **Keep balanced.** If your work, sport or other activities are very focused on exercising only one side of our body, your spine can be twisted, creating imbalances and constant twisting forces that can stress your spine and back muscles. For example, Tennis players or Golfers invariably have considerable body imbalances. The Tennis player will be much stronger at the shoulder, arm and across the entire region of the racquet side and Golfers train their body to only ever hit the ball to either the left or right, never both. To counteract this imbalance, they should focus on exercising the muscle groups on the opposite side, which will help keep the back and spine in alignment.

6. **Use your legs.** Your leg muscles are the strongest in your body and by utilising them when you need to bend up and down, you will avoid dangerously stressing your back. Always carry a load close to your body and seek assistance so that you never compromise your body position to move or lift an object.

Ensuring that your back is strong needn't take huge chunks out of your week and time spent on integrating simple exercises and movement patterns will be time well spent. You can be sure that you are taking positive steps to safeguarding your key supporting structure and you won't add to the statistic of 13 million working days lost each year due to back problems!

Basics

> *'Fitness has to do with the quality of life, not the quantity of it'.*
> ***George Sheehan***

The fitness recipe

Once you've decided that you're ready to start your fitness programme, what exactly should you be looking to do to get fit? A correctly balanced health and fitness programme should encompass Cardiovascular (CV), Strength, Flexibility and coordination training, supported by correct Nutrition. Omit one ingredient from the fitness recipe and the end result will be incomplete.

So, looking at these disciplines one-by-one, what should you be doing?

- **CV.** Your target should be a minimum of five CV sessions a week, each lasting up to one hour. CV training could be anything from brisk walking, through to running, rowing, cycling, specific gym CV machines or perhaps a recreational activity like dancing. Providing that the activity gets your heart pumping more than usual and you sustain it continuously, you can be confident that you're getting beneficial CV exercise. The key benefits are a strong engine and easy weight management.

- **Strength.** With strength training, aim for two sessions per week, focusing on an all over body programme, with particular attention paid to maintaining correct posture and realigning any postural problems that you may have developed. Modern lifestyles are responsible for a great many of the postural problems that people suffer from and correct assessment and remedial training can reverse them. The key benefits are the ability to carry out everyday tasks more easily and a toned body.

- **Flexibility.** Flexibility training won't help you lose weight or tone up but it will help correct bad posture, lengthen muscles, restore complete functional range of movement and last but by no means least, has a fantastic feel-good factor because it makes you loose and supple.

- **Coordination.** Being able to coordinate movements and activities is extremely important and fundamental to every movement that we make. A well balanced exercise programme should involve coordination training through a broad and continually varying range of

exercises. Additional training can be carried out through specific activities such as skipping and the majority of sports
.

- **Nutrition.** One of the most important pieces in your fitness jigsaw, a health and fitness programme without due consideration for correct nutrition is at best two steps forward and 1.99 steps back! Ignore diets and also the raft of celebrity endorsed fitness DVD's that surface annually and then gather dust. Instead, use your common sense and eat sensibly.

Put these five components together and you've got all the ingredients for a healthy lifestyle recipe, providing that they're kept in balance.

Are you all-round fit?

When the now retired seven times Tour De France champion cyclist Lance Armstrong completed the New York Marathon, he cited it *'as the hardest physical thing I've ever done',* once he'd caught his breath over the finish line. Now that's a pretty amazing statement from such an elite athlete as Armstrong; who famously survived cancer prior to his unsurpassed cycling achievements. Armstrong's time was well short of the winner's but was still extremely good – he just dipped under the magical three hour barrier for the 26.2 miles but for him to have replicated his cycling performances in the marathon, he would have needed to complete the race in less than two hours and ten minutes, which is the standard by which elite marathon runners are judged. This clearly illustrates that whilst he is super-fit, he's super-fit for a specific sport – cycling, rather than being 'all-round' fit.

All round fitness is the optimum way forward with your training programme because you achieve a balanced physique and are far less likely to suffer an overuse injury from continually concentrating on a single discipline. Hence it is important to incorporate as much variety into your fitness programme as possible so that your training remains balanced and provides all-round fitness benefits, which is far more effective long-term.

How to enjoy the benefits of 'all-round' fitness

- **Get balanced!** If you dedicate yourself to a single exercise discipline, over time, you develop postural and musculo-skeletal imbalances that can affect your health, mobility, flexibility and functionality. For example, runners are often lacking in upper body strength, which compromises their running form and makes them inefficient.

- **Get OUT of the gym!** A lot of people enjoy resistance training and are frequent visitors to the weights area in the gym. However, although they are building a strong, lean physique, their most important muscle in the body – the heart, is hardly getting a workout and hence their exercise programme is severely unbalanced. Without a strong cardiovascular system, your risk of developing coronary heart disease and associated problems increases, so it is vital to give your CV system a workout as well.

- **Get INTO the gym!** Similarly, cardiovascular training devotees such as rowers, cyclists, runners and swimmers, will benefit by adopting the reverse approach by supplementing their exercise programme with some time in the weights room. Then they will not only have a strong heart and lungs from their CV exercise, they will also have a well conditioned body to match. Studies have shown that a regular programme of resistance training will not detract from your CV performance, in fact it will actually enhance it, via greater movement economy and less local muscular resistance to fatigue, so ideally, look to incorporate two resistance training sessions into your weekly programme, covering the whole body.

- **Get coordinated!** A frequently neglected element of a training programme is balance and coordination – training your body to complete movements efficiently and under control. Elderly people often experience declining coordination, primarily as a result of inactivity and activities that maintain and enhance your coordination will bring about both performance improvements and general health and fitness benefits. To work on your coordination, practise exercises in an unstable environment such as substituting a stability ball for your usual weights bench as a platform or consider taking an exercise class that gets you continually changing direction, such as Step or Circuits. Alternatively, try a new activity such as a racquet sport or for the more adventurous, how about ice skating!

- **Get stretched out!** Lack of flexibility is a major cause of soft tissue injuries, postural problems and general bodily discomfort and without exception, everyone can benefit enormously from correctly prescribed developmental flexibility exercises to help their posture. Whether you're looking to gain an extra percentage improvement over a rival, aiming for longevity in your chosen sport, or you just want to feel relaxed without unwanted muscular tension, incorporating stretching exercises into your routine will work wonders.

Children & Fitness

> *'Children yearn to be active. To stymie that urge is a crime'.*
>
> **MIKE SEARLE**

For the children . . .

Where do your children typically hang out? Are their preferred play areas the bedroom and lounge, where PlayStations, televisions, computers and Xboxes live; or is the garden, park and local neighbourhood their domain for activities such as cycling, tree-climbing or gliding along on Heelys? Chances are the former is more popular than the latter, as we increasingly witness a spiral of *'static activities'* as opposed to *'active activities'* for our children. Why do I make that claim? Well, aside from my own observations of children's fitness, research has highlighted that less than 3% of 11-year old children are taking enough exercise to benefit their health. Breaking that down, a recently published study of 5,500 children found that only one in 250 girls and one in 20 boys are sufficiently active to maintain good health.

A team from Bath and Bristol University found that just 0.4% of girls and 5% of boys completed an hour of moderate to vigorous activity a day, at time when they should be most active both for their current health and fitness needs but also to cement healthy practices to carry through into adulthood. It appears that lifestyle changes and concerns about our children's freedom are conspiring to generate a situation which at the extreme end is predicted could result in the current generation of children being the first that are outlived by their parents. Fantasy and scaremongering? Well, again, it is being predicted that the obesity crisis will overwhelm the health service. Phrases such as *'contaminated childhood'* are being coined in the media as estimates suggest that because of these problems, in excess of 700,000 children are putting their future health at risk.

Okay, so that's the bad news, well what's the way forward? Not an easy nut to crack because we're now living in the 21st century, the era of technological revolution which continues to gather pace. In the space of a generation, our lives have changed immeasurably and the majority of those changes are here to stay, so it's no use lamenting the fewer opportunities to let children out alone, the fact that some two thirds of homes have a computer, etc, etc. We have to circumnavigate these problems and create opportunities for our children to enjoy current and long-term health benefits from regular activity.

No riches or material possessions can ever compensate for Illness, sickness or poor health and whilst children will typically think at their age that they're 'invincible', every adult knows that as each year passes, health and fitness issues become ever more important to us. With our technological lifestyles, any opportunity to help our children get fit, stay fit and reap the benefits of a healthy lifestyle have never been more important.

For the children.

Start as you mean to go on!

When you're younger, you can get away with a lot – late nights, little exercise and a poor diet – can't you? Well no, actually I'm afraid you can't because the latest statistics on children's health totally refutes that myth and makes for very alarming reading.

- Current estimates are that 20% of children are overweight.
- Obesity in children rose by over 40% between 1995 and 2003.
- 50% of children are predicted to be obese by 2020.
- The annual cost of obesity to the NHS is £1 billion.
- If obesity trends continue, this cost to the NHS will rise to £3.6 billion – within 4 years.

Am I obese?

A simple rule of thumb test to see if you're too overweight is to calculate your Body Mass Index (See the health status questionnaire at the beginning of this book for how to determine your BMI).

Obesity brings a whole host of lifestyle and health problems, including a higher risk of developing serious health problems in later life, such as heart disease, strokes, type 2 diabetes, bowel cancer and high blood pressure; with the risk of health problems increasing the more overweight someone becomes.

Below are the top six self-help strategies and ideas that can inspire your children to get involved in healthy activities which will hopefully carry over into their adult lives.

Top 6 Tips to keep your children healthy

1. **What do you do?** You can hardly expect your kids to toe the health and fitness line if you aren't setting a good example yourself. Children often mimic their parent's behaviour and want to get involved in what you're doing, so if you're eating healthily and exercising, your children are more likely to follow suit.

2. **Normal limits apply!** Hours spent in front of the TV / DVD / PlayStation does nothing for your child's physical development. However, confiscating them completely is unreasonable so why not set some limits on viewing/playing time to get a balance between sedentary and active pursuits.

3. **Go clubbing!** A sports club is a great way for your child to get involved in activities, week in, week out. Clubs are always on the lookout for new talent, there's a club out there to suit everyone and your child will meet lots of new friends too.

4. **Make food interesting!** Kids can typically be extremely fickle when it comes to food but simple strategies such as mixing up colourful salads, chopping up raw vegetables like carrots for snacks and packing grapes in a lunchbox instead of biscuits are cheap and cheerful solutions that children will enjoy.

5. **Keep everything fun!** Nothing will turn your kids off more than if they feel that they are being surreptitiously coerced into something, so make sure that the fun element remains. Ideas include family activities such as swimming, cycling or walking, or perhaps outdoor family games – and if Mum and Dad don't score too highly, the kids will be really enthused!

6. **Get a role model.** The media is overflowing with great role models for children to identify with and many a current star has cited their inspiration as watching a sporting hero as a child and of course, to be a top sports star – you have to be healthy!

Christmas

> *'I always trained on Christmas Day because my rivals weren't.*
> ***DALEY THOMPSON, DOUBLE OLYMPIC GOLD MEDALLIST***

How big is YOUR Christmas dinner?

Everyone eagerly anticipates their Christmas dinner – traditionally, the centrepiece of the day. Christmas is a time for families and celebrating and I for one would not wish to put a dampener on the festive proceedings by suggesting complete abstinence from culinary attractions over the holiday period. A typical Christmas dinner is usually a highly calorie laden affair but calorie counting is a very negative way to look at food intake. A far better approach is to focus on a sustainable healthy lifestyle encompassing an unprocessed nutrition plan and regular exercise.

However, just how many calories could you consume on Christmas Day and how can you balance that with some lower calorie ideas and alternatives that will not spoil your enjoyment of the big day but will help to lighten the load a little, something that your waistline will be grateful for when you ring in the New Year!

Christmas Day calories

1. **Breakfast.** Scrambled eggs on toast, fruit juice, tea or coffee with milk – approx 400 calories.

2. **Mid-morning.** Two pints of beer or other alcoholic equivalents – approx 400 calories.

3. **Christmas Dinner.** Roast turkey and all the trimmings + wine – approx 1,500 calories.

   Christmas pudding, cream / brandy butter – approx 700 calories

   Cheese and biscuits – 400 calories

   Mince pies, cream, chocolates – approx 1,000 calories

4. **Snacks.** Crisps, nuts, dates, sweets, etc – approx 1,000 calories.

5. **Evening.** Turkey sandwiches, Christmas cake, beer / wine, etc – approx 1,000 calories.

All that adds up to a massive 6,400 calories – and that doesn't include typically generous portions and home measures for alcoholic drinks! When you consider that an average person needs between 2000 and 2,500 calories per day if they aren't being particularly active, then you're left with an excess of approximately 4,000 calories which is equivalent to more than an entire pound of body-fat and that's just looking at one day! Factor in replicating the experience at Christmas parties, family entertaining and lower levels of activity and it's no surprise that January can be a time to refocus on your fitness goals!

However, by making just a few simple adjustments, you can still enjoy everything on Christmas Day but with far fewer calories. . !

Christmas Day calorie savers.

1. **Drinking.** Alcohol is a real calorie culprit but if you simply alternate your drinks with water, you'll easily halve your calorie intake and you'll also enjoy feeling much better throughout the day. Additionally on Boxing Day morning your head will thank you as well! *Saving = 700 calories.*

2. **Christmas Dinner.** Omit bacon and sausages from the main course, swap cream / brandy butter for low fat crème fraiche or custard made with semi-skimmed milk, try high cocoa chocolate instead of confectionary which will reduce your sugar craving and forget about mince pies at the end of the meal (haven't you had enough of them by Christmas Day!). Also put plenty of vegetables on your plate, which will give you a good dose of fibre, leaving you feeling fuller for longer. Opt for low fat cheeses such as Edam or simply reduced fat alternatives to popular makes and swap high fat crackers for oat biscuits or just leave them out altogether.
Saving = 1,200 calories.

3. **Snacks.** Freshen up your taste buds with a fruit platter or a bunch of grapes instead of high fat crisps and nuts and the natural fruit sugars will also stem any craving that you may have for sweets as well. *Saving = 700 calories.*

4. **Exercise.** Why not enjoy a brisk family walk either before or after your Christmas dinner, which could consume several hundred calories and elevate your metabolic rate for several hours afterwards which will further increase your calorie burn. Christmas Day is a great day to get out and about because it's so quiet with minimal traffic and a pre-lunch session will help you enjoy your dinner more. *Saving =400 calories.*

So with just a few minor – but very effective changes, you can save approximately 3,000 calories, which is nearly half of the potentially massive calorie consumption on Christmas Day!

Of course Christmas isn't confined to a single day. Boxing Day often sees the whole shebang repeated at another family member's home, so if you haven't found time for a workout, Boxing Day is a good time. Most gyms will be open on Boxing Day so try and do a composite session that includes both cardiovascular and resistance training exercises because then you're far more likely to get an all-over body workout, which is more effective at calorie burning than concentrating on a single exercise discipline.

SuperTip

Research by the British Heart Foundation has found that a long walk before a fat-laden Christmas dinner can significantly help to balance out the excesses. Walking for 90 minutes improves the function of the blood vessels and also lowers blood fat levels, with the benefits lasting well into Boxing Day. 90 minutes may be difficult to fit into a busy day but as long as you get out and make your walk brisk, you'll still enjoy some of those same benefits.

Cheers!

Echoing around pubs, clubs, bars, parties in December is a chorus of *'cheers, good health, bottoms up'* etc as everyone gets into the festive spirit and enjoys a few drinks with friends. Whether you're a very occasional drinker or you regularly enjoy a few pints, there's no doubt about it, Christmas is a time of increased alcohol consumption for a great many people.

Debates on the benefits of consuming alcohol will run and run and the focus here is not to add to that topic of discussion but rather to introduce some festive drinking tips which will help you both enjoy the party season without suffering the following day!

Festive drinking tips

1. **Know your units!** To begin with, it is helpful to know just what the suggested maximum weekly alcohol consumption is for men and

women. The latest recommendations are that men consume no more than 14 units per week and women 7 units. A unit is approximately equivalent to ½ a pint of standard strength beer, a single measure of spirits or a small glass of wine. Women have a smaller allowance because typically their bodies are smaller. The male body is 66% fluid and the female 55% so any alcohol consumed by a woman is less diluted in the body and hence they tend to get drunk quicker on the same amount of alcohol!

2. **Watch those home measures!** The unit measures above refer to standard pub measures. However, when dispensing drinks at home, everyone tends to be more generous! A single whiskey quickly becomes a double and a large wine glass can easily contain two units! Add frequent top-ups into the equation and before you know it, you're up to half your weekly consumption so keep an eye on generous hosts!

3. **Alternate your drinks.** Alcohol is a diuretic which means it causes you to lose more fluid from the body than you consume. After an evening's drinking, your whole body can be dehydrated, particularly your brain, which accounts for that thumping headache the following morning if you've had a few too many. To help last the evening, try alternating alcoholic drinks with soft drinks or water so that you maintain your fluid levels.

4. **Eat, eat, eat!** If you know that you're likely to drink more than usual, always try and combine alcohol with food so effectively you have something to soak it all up. This will have the effect of slowing down the rate at which alcohol enters the bloodstream so that you're less likely to feel unwell.

5. **Stick to what you know!** It's an old adage but try and avoid mixing your drinks. Alcohol is a toxin to the body and consuming a cocktail of different types means that your body has to work that much harder in trying to deal with them all.

6. **Pace yourself.** Try and avoid that initial rush where you down the first couple of drinks rapidly – and often feel the effects rapidly too! Your body can only process alcohol at the rate of one unit per hour so if you're out for the evening, it's likely that you can only get rid of 4-6 units. The more you consume, the more the effects (particularly the following day!) will hit you, so try and pace your drinking.

7. **A hair of the dog doesn't work.** It's a very old remedy when you're feeling the effects of the night before to kick-start your body

with another alcoholic drink. However, you're actually just adding to your levels of dehydration and toxins and further delaying your 'alcohol comedown'. Instead, drink as much water as possible, which is the best way of returning your body to a healthy balance.

8. **Take a day off!** Unfortunately that doesn't mean from work, it means from drinking! It's easy to get hooked into a cycle of going out night after night or uncorking the bottle as soon as you step in through the front door. Try having an alcohol free day each week to allow your body to recover from the effects of drinking.

All these Festive Drinking Tips are designed to help you enjoy the festive celebrations rather than preach about any harmful effects from alcohol consumption. Everyone knows that drinking to excess is damaging, instead, simply combine these tips with a few units of commonsense and you can both enjoy a drink and keep a healthy balance in your life.

SuperTip

Unsure of how many units are in your drink?

Simply multiply the alcohol percentage by the drink volume in millilitres and then divide the lot by 1,000 to find out how many units you're drinking.

Eg: A 750ml bottle of wine with an alcohol percentage of 12.5% contains 9.4 units.

That's

$$\frac{750 \times 12.5}{1{,}000} = 9.4 \text{ units of alcohol}$$

Core Training

'Your core is your body's chassis. A weak core equals a weak body'.
MIKE SEARLE

Core! Core! Core!

Imagine trying to fire a cannon from a canoe and then successfully hitting a target - a pretty difficult task I'm sure you'll agree. Obviously the task is difficult because the floating canoe is a very unstable platform, which will result in the cannon moving around all over the place, especially when it fires. And what do canoes have to do with a fitness programme you're probably thinking.

Core stability exercises are exercises which create a *'stable platform'* within your body. By applying the same logic as the example of the canoe to our bodies, if your own *'platform'* is similarly unstable, then all your movements are less efficient, your posture is poor and your strength reduced. Whatever activity or sport you are involved in, time spent enhancing your core strength will bring about tremendous benefits in terms of improved posture and performance.

So what parts of the body do we mean when we refer to core stability muscles? The best way to think of your core muscles is to imagine a corset that wraps right around your body, from underneath your ribcage, right down to your pelvic floor (which holds your intestines etc in place). However, these muscles aren't visible like the proverbial 'six-pack'. They are deep postural muscles that hold us in, provide support and keep us upright but just because they aren't visible like a six-pack, doesn't mean that they aren't important – in fact they are absolutely vital. These muscles often become de-trained, resulting in poor posture and an overall weakness in the body. Thankfully there is a solution and not only can core muscles be 're-trained', the benefits and effects are rapid and the process can be good fun too! All-in-all, a good package of reasons to include them in your fitness programme.

With good core stability, you can activate these core muscles in both specific core exercises to improve their strength but also in everyday activities like walking down the street with good posture. Think about how the muscles of your neck constantly support your head – without you being aware that they're actually working. That is how you want your core muscles to work, maintaining good posture automatically.

The range of core exercises that you can do is immense but extremely worthwhile on your road to improved core strength and posture and overall total body efficiency.

Starting core training

1. **Get a stability ball.** Stability balls, Swiss balls, fit-balls, core balls; all different names for the large balls that you can buy in the High Street and find in good gyms. Inexpensive and good fun to use, a Stability Ball is a key weapon in your core training arsenal.

2. **Locate your core.** Next, you need to find your core muscles and learn how to activate them. Stand upright in a relaxed position, and position two fingers of one hand above and below your navel. Try and lift one leg off the floor without shifting your bodyweight. As you begin to move, you should feel your core muscles switch on, stabilising your body as you try to lift your leg. The core contraction that you make and feel when you lift your leg is the same contraction needed during core exercises.

3. **Get on the ball!** Use your stability ball frequently. Simply sitting on your ball will strengthen core muscles and there are opportunities to use it throughout the day. A few minutes whilst you're watching TV, working on the computer, even eating a meal will all contribute to training your core muscles and dramatically improving your posture.

4. **Try a core exercise.** A great foundation core exercise using a stability ball is to lie on the floor on your back with your heels on the centre of the ball. Slowly raise your pelvis until you form a straight line through your shoulders, hips and ankles. Maintaining your balance will challenge your core muscles extremely effectively and you should aim to build up to 60 seconds in the position.

5. **Keep breathing!** With the concentration and strong muscle contractions that core training requires, it's very easy to hold your breath as you focus on balance and stability. Avoid holding your breath, just breathe normally because if you forget to breathe, you can send your blood pressure up, which is undesirable.

6. **Practise what you practice!** Don't let your core training end when you put your stability ball away. Your specific core training should be just the beginning. Once you have found and can activate your core, use these tools in your everyday life. Eg: when you go to lift a weight, contract your core so that you strengthen your whole body. When you're walking around, activate your core so that you maintain good posture. Soon you'll find that using your core becomes automatic and you will be walking tall, looking slimmer and people will comment on your improved posture and shape.

Cross Training

'Variety is the spice of life'. **WILLIAM COWPER**

Mix up your fitness!

I am frequently asked to recommend the most suitable exercises for children and I always advise that the ideal solution is to ensure that children always have plenty of variety and that they participate in a broad range of activities in order to fully support their physical development. Additionally, it is equally important to keep all their games and activities fun; rather than try and impose any form of rigid training routine because too much formal structure is more likely to turn a child away from fitness than encourage them to keep fit and healthy. Of course, what I am effectively recommending is *'cross-training'* which is today's terminology for mixing up your exercise routine to maintain interest, motivation and progression.

Cross-training is a great strategy for avoiding injuries, freshening up your workouts and getting greater all-round and long-term fitness gains, so by *'Mixing up your Fitness'* you get more from your workouts.

Top 5 cross-training tips & benefits

1. **Easier weight management.** If you always limit yourself to a single form of exercise, you only ever use the same muscle groups. However, if you continually vary your sessions, you will use a much wider range of muscles and research has shown that this keeps your metabolic rate at a higher level. The end result is that you burn more calories, making weight management much easier to achieve.

2. **Reduced injury risk.** If your exercise programme is correctly prescribed and balanced and you follow correct training protocols, your incidence of injury should be extremely low. However, many people only ever carry out one form of exercise and runners are a prime example. If you only ever run, imbalances can occur within the body and the repetitious nature of doing the same actions many thousands of times can result in injury. Running is a fantastic activity and strengthens the cardiovascular system and legs – but not much else. Hence, following a structured *'all-over-body'* exercise programme will keep you balanced and out of the sports therapist's treatment room.

3. **Maximum motivation!** If I had £1 for everyone that had told me that exercise was boring, that villa in the south of France would now be a reality! Frequently, people become bored with exercise because they do boring exercise. Always carrying out the same sessions on the same equipment in the same location IS BORING! So, don't get stuck in a rut, mix up your training and breathe new life into your workouts!

4. **Cardiovascular AND resistance training.** With regard to their exercise habits, a lot of people fall into one of two camps. Either they do CV workouts or they lift weights and it can be hard to find someone that does both. However, doing both is exactly the right exercise prescription because for long term health and fitness, it is important to address all your fitness needs, not just a single area. Think of your body as a composite piece rather than separate elements such as a CV system and muscles. Every sport and activity employs a combination of physical requirements and so focusing on just one doesn't provide you with long-term health and fitness benefits.

5. **Improved fitness.** Another great benefit of cross-training is that you actually get fitter for your favourite sport. So after a hard run, you won't want a tough session the next day but you can enjoy a quality weights session the day after which will improve your all-round strength whilst still allowing your body to recover from the demands of your previous running workout. The end result is that you get stronger which can then be converted into improved race performances.

So, lose weight, stay injury free, have fun, balance your body and get fitter; all by introducing some variety into your exercise sessions and *'mixing up your fitness'.*

Cycling

> *'Nothing compares to the simple pleasure of a bike ride'.*
> ***JOHN F. KENNEDY***

Get on your bike!

For anyone looking to exercise their heart and lungs, there are many different ways of getting a cardiovascular workout and there is no definitive 'best' or 'worst' method. However, if you're looking for a low impact, time-saving fitness solution, you would have to go a long way to beat cycling. Almost everyone owns a bicycle (and knows how to ride one!) and it offers a cheap way of increasing your fitness levels.

Less than 1½ % of all journeys in this country are made by bike but with an increasing number of cycling-friendly strategies including dedicated cycle lanes, cycling is safe, good fun and great exercise. To support that statement, let's focus upon the benefits of cycling which might just encourage you to 'get on your bike!'

'Get on your bike' cycling benefits

- **Easier weight management.** Increased levels of activity = increased calorie burn. Therefore, if you are more active through cycling, your chances of unwanted weight gain are less. For example, a short 20 minute cycle ride to and from work each day burns the equivalent of 2 pounds of fat a month, or 1½ stones each year!

- **Psychological boost!** A further benefit of cardiovascular exercise is that it improves your mood. Cardiovascular exercise releases feel-good chemicals in the brain known as endorphins and hence your stress levels are reduced. This feel-good factor occurs both during and for a long time after your cycle ride, so you'll arrive in work with a spring in your step!

- **Reduced risk of heart disease.** To exercise your heart and lungs, you need to use large muscle groups to create a demand for oxygen. Your largest muscles are in your legs, so cycling is certain to get your heart rate going. If you follow a regular programme of cycling, studies have shown that you can lower your risk of heart disease by as much as 22%.

- **Time Saver.** Now this one benefits everyone. We're all busy with work, family and other commitments and sometimes, finding the time for exercise can be difficult. However, there are few better opportunities to combine commuting with exercise than with cycling and you may find that your journey times are shorter because you can zip through the rush-hour with ease!

- **Kinder to your pocket!** Bikes are cheap to buy and run requiring no tax, insurance or MOT and servicing costs are a fraction of car maintenance bills – even cheaper if you do it yourself, which isn't too difficult. Parking is free and the average bike lasts much longer than a car.

SuperTip

Do you often come down with colds and viruses? Weak immune systems result in a greater susceptibility to infections but a regular exercise programme will boost your body's natural defences against illness. Cycling has been shown to be one of the most effective ways of improving the quality of your immune system, which means you're improving the quality of your life as well!

Back in the saddle

If you fancy getting cycle-fit; follow these beginners cycling training tips which might just tempt you back into the saddle. . !

Top 5 beginning cycling training tips

1. **Take the long way home!** The foundation of all your cycling training should be a weekly long ride. Long can mean anything from a few miles to a ride lasting many hours, depending upon your goals but it is essential for building basic endurance. Look to gradually increase your distance rather than ramp it up very quickly, which is likely to result in muscle soreness, excessive fatigue and possibly injury. The better job you do of building this

foundation, the better the results will be from your faster paced training. Your long ride isn't a race or time-trial, it's a more comfortably paced session, focusing more on 'time in the saddle' rather than speed.

2. **Speed it up!** Following your base building period, the next step is to cycle faster. Always precede a faster paced session by a few miles of easier riding so that you are thoroughly warmed up; even in the summer months. Try alternating 10 minute faster bursts with 4 minute recoveries, followed by some easy spinning of the pedals for a few miles to cool down. Alternatively, go out with a few friends and each of you take it in turns to set a faster pace before dropping back for the next rider to take over. The overall pace of the group will be faster and you get your 'rest period' slipstreaming behind the other riders, working harder when it's your turn at the front.

3. **Climb every mountain!** Hill climbing is effectively speed work in disguise because although your speed will be slower on the hills, your CV system is getting as a good a workout (if not better in some cases) as when you're cycling on more level ground. The additional benefit with hills is that you build leg strength which will serve you well whatever topography you encounter. Try cycling around an undulating course, working hard on each hill climb and you'll rapidly improve. Alternatively, pick a challenging hill and complete a session of 6-10 hard ascents, turning at the top and recovering on the way down.

4. **Stretch out!** One element of your training should not take place on the bike at all – and that's flexibility exercises. Bent over on a bike for long periods can result in over-stretched upper back muscles and a tight chest. Additionally, with all the exercise that your legs get, regular stretching is important to helping them keep injury free, loose and supple. Try and stretch your legs after EVERY ride and your arms and chest twice a week.

5. **Poor weather options.** Although the summer should be blessed with good weather, there are no guarantees in an English summer so if the weather takes a turn for the worse, there are still alternatives to help you maintain your cycling fitness. Spinning classes at the gym provide a fun, challenging, group-based session on stationary bikes that is effectively a hill climbing and interval session rolled into one – so it's a great cycling workout. You might also like to try a cycle trainer, which fixes to your back wheel and allows you to train indoors such as in your garage whilst your bike is supported on a stand.

Diets

'The definition of the word diet has been corrupted to mean what not to eat'. ***MIKE SEARLE***

The breakthrough diet!

Every couple of months there is a news story that centres on an AMAZING weight-loss solution such as the 'Diet Drug' that *'fools the stomach into feeling full'.* Scientists working at Imperial College, London, have discovered a naturally occurring digestive hormone in the small intestine, which when injected into the body, increases levels of another chemical that tells your brain you're full. The idea is that you then no longer overeat and weight-loss can occur. Initial experiments have been positive and surprise, surprise, a Professor on the research team has formed a company to potentially market a product in the future.

Oh dear, here we go again. The merry-go-round of weight-loss strategies continues unabated. Not so long ago we were bombarded with information about Leptin, a naturally occurring chemical in our own bodies that helps to regulate appetite. We were told how experiments with fat mice and Leptin had produced encouraging results. You may have heard of the drug Xenical, which changes the way that fat is digested in the body by preventing its absorption. Unfortunately, users of Xenical find the side effects of taking the drug difficult to manage – you suffer from severe diarrhoea if you consume any fat at all in your diet! Further scientific diet strategies have involved modifying foods so that they are 'fat free'. Olestra was developed as a fat that couldn't be absorbed and also resulted in diarrhoea, in addition to inhibiting the absorption of other important nutrients. Other diet drugs have had to be withdrawn after widespread use uncovered serious side effects including conditions like primary pulmonary hypertension, a constriction of the blood vessels which can cause widespread tissue damage leading to death.

Equally well-known and publicised weight-loss solutions include stomach stapling, surgery and the never ending round of diets and diet products available in the High Street. Many a fashion magazine can be found espousing how the latest celebrity has lost untold pounds by following a miracle new diet regime. Advertised products and services are everywhere; including tablets, slimming clubs, supplements, creams, diet foods, body belts, special clothing, books, DVD's, etc, etc. The truth is:

THE DIET INDUSTRY GROWS FATTER BY SELLING DREAMS OF THINNESS BUT DELIVERS ONLY FAILURE.

If any of these methods worked, all the others would be put out of business overnight – but the multi-million pound diet industry shows no sign of slowing down.

There is a huge and continual interest in weight-loss and dieting but with unsustainable results, so what actually is the solution to maintaining a healthy weight and much more importantly; a healthy lifestyle. With an estimated 50% of the population overweight and with obesity levels approaching 25%, the evidence and statistics demonstrate that diets don't work.

All the leading experts on health and nutrition are recognising that developing long-term healthy strategies for life that involve regular exercise are essential for our future health. My solution for successful weight management is straightforward. My fantastic weight-management product can make you leaner, lighter, stronger, firmer, more flexible, more agile, more energetic, more confident, increases alertness, is fun and motivating and delivers long-lasting results! Diets must be the ultimate example of over-promising and under-delivering but my breakthrough diet solution is a healthy, balanced and correctly prescribed exercise programme, combined with sensible eating.

SuperTip

Throw away your diet books! Instead of depriving yourself of food, change your focus and seek out ways of burning more calories each day. Weight management is a straightforward equation. What goes in (Food) must equal what's used up (Energy), or else weight gain occurs. To kick-start your plan, think how many times in the last week you used the car for a journey that you could have easily done on foot – and burnt more calories. How about occasionally ditching the car, walking, getting fitter and losing weight all rolled into one!

Diets make you FAT!

At last! It's official! Following a study from scientific researchers at the University of California, their findings have determined that diets of any kind make you fat. So whether it's Atkins, cabbage soup, grapefruit, Hay, Macrobiotic, F-Plan, Beverley Hills, Mayo, Zone, Lo-carb or any of the multitude of quick-fix weight management solutions that have gone in and out of favour across the decades; the bottom line (excuse the pun) is that they're all a waste of time. Now I'm sure that many readers will be thinking – just wait a minute, I was on such-and-such a diet and lost X pounds but the real question is: for how long did those pounds stay off? In the 21st century, weight loss is a major issue and problem and people need a solution but the dieting solution isn't effective.

To help illustrate the point, consider the following 12 stage process which details exactly what actually happens to your body when you go on a diet, together with the solution for long-term weight management.

Why diets make you fat – the 12 step process.

1. Initially when you embark on a 'new' diet, you are full of enthusiasm and highly motivated to achieve weight loss. This carries you through the early days and sometimes weeks, even though at times you may find the diet difficult but you steal yourself against those hunger pangs and 'tough it out'.

2. After a week or two – or indeed with some diets, after only a matter of days, you find that you've lost some weight, which confirms that the diet is working and helps maintain your motivation to continue. Result!

3. However, the vast majority of diets and indeed dieters seek rapid results, ie: weight loss of more than 1-1½ pounds per week. A reduction of 1 pound doesn't look very impressive when you step onto the scales and doesn't give you much of a tangible result for all your gritty abstinence, whereas a serious loss of several pounds is far more motivating. Unfortunately therein lies the problem.

4. When you lose weight at too rapid a rate, you lose water, body-fat and also lean muscle. Lean muscle is a calorie burner (every pound of lean muscle burns an extra 50 calories a day) and so as your muscle mass drops, so does your metabolic rate (the speed at which you burn calories).

5. Additionally because you are effectively putting your body into 'famine mode', your body identifies that for life preservation, it needs to slow your metabolic rate.

6. This double hit on the rate at which you burn calories causes your weight loss to plateau and stop. The diet really starts to bite now and you find it increasingly difficult to maintain your motivation to continue because your body is sending you all the opposite signals to break out of the famine.

7. Eventually you stop the diet, usually having achieved some weight loss, so you feel that the short-term hit has had some effect.

8. Having come off the diet, you resume your pre-diet eating plan – the plan which originally contributed to your desire to lose weight.

9. Once you start eating normally again, your body recognises that famine mode is over and as a self preservation strategy, tries to ensure that should the famine recur, it will be better prepared. Hence of the calories you consume, more are stored as body-fat in case the famine returns.

10. This fat storage is compounded by the fact that because your muscle mass has dropped due to the too rapid weight loss, your daily calorie burn is less than pre-diet and this contributes to further fat storage.

11. The end result is that at some point after you stop the diet, you find that the weight has gone back on – and some more (the famine protection system). Of course this is extremely de-motivating after all your hard efforts and at some point later, you may be tempted to try a different diet . . .

12. Unfortunately, the dieting cycle then repeats.

The 12 point plan will be familiar to many readers – of course the question is – if diets make you fat then how can you keep your weight in check.

My favourite equation is calories in, minus energy expenditure = zero.

So if you burn up what you eat, your weight will remain constant. Equally if you burn up more than you consume, your weight must fall. Of course burning up calories via exercise isn't the full picture because for sustainable weight management, your exercise must be supported by healthy eating, which means portion control, whole-foods and limiting the bad guys – energy dense yet nutritionally poor foods such as confectionary products.

However, that has to be more attractive than a depressing repeat cycle of weight on, weight off and that continual focus on calories that dieters endure.

Trapped in the dieting cycle?

Now runners are not known for their bulky, muscular physiques; rather for having a good engine and an ability to run far and fast. In fact a great many of them would benefit from specific training to build both core and total body strength because you actually run with your whole body, not just your legs and runners often neglect overall conditioning and are *'too thin to win'*. Overall conditioning is extremely important for runners – and everyone else as well because for all round health and fitness, exercising to maintain strength and muscle mass will counteract and even reverse the decline that occurs as we age.

Many non-runners are also *'too thin to win'* because they have spent years trapped in the dieting cycle and the end result is that they have stripped out muscle mass and hence have developed postural problems. Additionally because they have lost a lot of muscle, their daily calorie burn is reduced because carrying some muscle increases the number of calories that your body uses. A reduced calorie burn encourages them to diet even more to maintain their shape and they become trapped in *'the dieting cycle'*. This cycle can be very difficult to break but by prescribing correct training together with nutritional analysis you can avoid falling into this trap.

How to avoid the dieting cycle

1. **Don't miss a meal.** Often, when trying to lose weight, people will skip meals in the hope that reducing their calorie intake will result in weight loss. Eating less will result in weight loss but it is important to still eat regular meals because otherwise your body will think it is in starvation mode and will conserve energy – stalling your weight loss.

2. **Lift weights.** By exercising with weights, you will keep your muscles toned up. This not only keeps you looking in great shape, it also means that your metabolic rate (the speed at which you burn calories) is elevated; whether you are exercising or not. The end result is a greater calorie burn all day, every day.

3. **Slowly, slowly, slowly.** If you are trying to lose weight, avoid trying to lose it quickly. Everyone wants instant results but rapid weight loss will ultimately lead to rapid weight gain a little further down the line. Instead, look to lose 1 to 1½ pounds per week and you will find that although the weight comes off gradually, it stays off – long-term.

4. **Cardiovascular training works!** An exercise session that works your heart and lungs will not only burn calories whilst you exercise but also for a period of time after you've finished. The more intense

the activity, the greater the post-exercise calorie burn. Look to train for 30 minutes to an hour and you'll get real results.

5. **Don't count calories.** There can be few more pointless skills than being able to look at a plate of food and know how many calories it contains. Counting calories results in food issues totally dominating your life which is extremely negative. Instead, improve your knowledge of healthy and non-healthy foods and focus on eating the former instead of the latter. Easy wins include ditching processed, high fat and high sugar foods in favour of natural foods such as fruit and vegetables.

The simple fact is that diets don't work – they never have, or else purveyors of whatever is the latest *'new diet system'* would be out of a job. Correctly prescribed, regular exercise, combined with whole-food nutrition is the way forward so that you're never again *'trapped in the dieting cycle'.*

SuperTip

If you're thinking about starting a diet, perhaps to lose some weight for your summer holidays, DON'T! Instead, take the long-term view and consider taking some positive steps to improving your health and fitness for life, not just for a fortnight in the sun.

Exercise with a Disability

> *'The race we are running is against our weaker selves'.*
> **BRUCE TULLOH, EUROPEAN 5000 METRES GOLD MEDALLIST**

Exercise for all!

Structured exercise with a focus on ensuring that your training programme keeps your body in balance is essential. However, for some people that can prove particularly difficult if for example you are disabled or perhaps you're suffering from an injury. If you fall into either of those two categories, it's easy to think that exercise isn't for you or it's too difficult to work out but exercise should be and is for everyone. There are over 8.5 million disabled people in the UK and although this includes all disabilities, physically disabled people make up a high proportion of that figure.

If you suffer from a disability or perhaps are unable to carry out some movements, follow the exercise ideas below which will help you get started in fitness, feel better and will make a positive contribution to your overall health.

Fitness with a disability tips

1. **Book a check-up with your GP.** Before you embark on your fitness programme talk to your GP. Your Doctor will welcome your plans and will be able to advise you on any specific precautions that you should take, relevant to your condition.

2. **Focus on what you CAN do.** There are likely to be certain exercises, movements and activities that you cannot do because of your disability. Rather than focus on what you can't do, put your efforts into what you can achieve. Very few of us can become Olympic Champions but we can all do the best with what we have.

3. **Choose activities which you enjoy.** Irrespective of specific benefits from specific activities, select activities that give you a buzz because you're more likely to continue with them long term. A regular exercise programme has psychological benefits as well as physical ones and you're unlikely to get that *'feel-good factor'* if you're not enjoying your training.

4. **Get professional advice.** Seek out an exercise professional who can provide quality, experienced input into your plans so that you get the maximum benefits from the exercises that you can do.

5. **Work on your weaknesses.** If you don't know what you need to do, you won't get benefits from your training, so it is important that your specific needs are assessed and that your exercise programme is targeted at maintaining and improving key areas that will add quality to your life.

6. **Don't go it alone.** Coping with a disability is challenging enough, let alone maintaining your motivation week in, week out. Training continuity is key, so try to link up with someone for training like your partner or a friend, who can help and support you.

7. **Think positive!** There may be many things that you can't do but there will certainly be many things that you can. For example, if you're a wheelchair user, you can use hand cycles and do upper body exercises. If you have a co-ordination disability then you can still do seated exercises etc. Maintain a positive outlook and you will get more out of your workout and progress faster.

8. **Access for all.** Legislation has resulted in better access for disabled people and that includes gymnasiums so there are many opportunities to work out in the gym if you have a disability but if that proves impractical, you can still exercise in the comfort of your own home and get stronger, fitter and improve the quality of your life.

Everyone should be involved in exercise that is suitable for them and structured around their personal health and fitness goals – after all, why should someone with a disability be excluded from health and fitness benefits?

Exercise ***is for all*** and will improve the quality of your life, whatever your current fitness levels or constraints.

Fitness Assessment

> *'When you are fit you fill your day. When you are unfit, you kill it'.*
> **GEORGE SHEEHAN**

Are you doing enough?

Gymnasiums and Leisure Clubs with bulging memberships, an explosion in mass participation road-running races, the *'5-a-day'* culture – surely that all means that as a nation we're more focused than ever on our health and well-being? Well actually I don't think that we are. Yes, there are ever more opportunities to keep fit and healthy with the proliferation of leisure facilities and the frequent media focus upon general health and fitness issues but that doesn't necessarily equate to an all-round healthier and fitter population. From my experience, there is generally a greater awareness of fitness issues but overall decreasing levels of fitness from the very young through to the elderly – which presents a worrying picture.

To illustrate my point, take the following quick quiz to check out your personal health and fitness scores.

Fitness health-check quick quiz

1. How many times per week are you involved in non-stop cardiovascular exercise (exercise that leaves you slightly breathless and gets your heart pumping), that lasts for a minimum of 30 minutes? *Score 1 point for each session.*

2. How many times per week do you exercise all the major muscles around your body, either as a specific resistance training workout or through other activities such as your work? *Score 1 point for each session.*

3. How many times per week do you follow a stretching programme which targets all the primary muscles around your body? *Score 1 point for each session.*

4. How many times per week are you able to find time specifically for yourself, where you can properly relax without distraction or stress from the telephone etc? *Score 1 point for each session.*

5. How many times per week do you skip a meal (eg: breakfast). *Deduct 1 point for each missed meal.*

6. How many times per week do you eat a meal that you know is either nutritionally poor or contributes little to your health (eg: takeaways)? *Deduct 1 point for each poor meal.*

7. Are you a smoker? *Yes - Deduct 1 point.*

8. Do you consume at least 2 litres of non-diuretic type fluids each day? (Drinks such as tea, coffee, cola and alcohol all contain caffeine which is a diuretic and dehydrates the body). *No - Deduct 1 point.*

9. Do you drink more than 14 units of alcohol (7 units for women) per week? *Yes - Deduct 1 point.*

10. Is your Body Mass Index (BMI) greater than 25? (See the health status questionnaire at the beginning of this book to determine your BMI). *BMI greater than 25 – Deduct 1 point.*

Results

So how did you score? Obviously this is a brief quiz but it is still very effective at providing an all round indicator of your general health and fitness.

- **Less than 10 points** – your health and fitness routine is out of balance. And it's as simple as that. There's no good/average/poor/needs attention, etc with this quiz because with your health and fitness there can be no compromise and no half measures. Either you're fit and healthy or you're not. Full stop.

The way forward

OK, so if you didn't achieve optimum scores, what should you be looking for to boost your totals?

1. Cardiovascular fitness – 5 sessions per week, each session lasting between 30 minutes and one hour.

2. Resistance training – 2 sessions per week, targeting all the major muscle groups around the body.

3. Flexibility – 2 sessions each week stretching all your primary muscles.

4. Time for you – at least once per week.

5. Missed meals (particularly breakfast) – never.

6. Consuming poor quality meals – never.

7. Smoking – no.

8. Fluid consumption – minimum of 2 litres per day, more in hot conditions and when exercising.

9. Alcohol – within the 14 units (men) and 7 units (women) limits.

10. BMI – in the range 20-25

Flexibility

> *'Stretching is the forgotten component of fitness'.* **MIKE SEARLE**

Stretcher case!

An appropriately prescribed selection of stretching exercises should be fundamental to any fitness programme but it is common to think of any form of fitness training as exercise that involves getting hot and sweaty such as running or gym work and forgo flexibility training in favour of more CV or weight exercises. Flexibility training doesn't get your heart rate up or build muscle but it's no less important – in fact it is equally important. If you are inflexible, your muscles are operating less functionally, your range of movement is reduced, you are more prone to injury when exercising and your posture is compromised – all factors which have long-term damaging effects upon the body. All is not lost though! By stretching regularly, you can maintain (and if utilising the correct techniques) even increase your flexibility and significantly reduce or prevent the problems above. Additionally, being supple and loose comes with an automatic 'feel-good factor' as everyday tasks become easier and less of a strain. No struggling to get up from the floor is one relevant benefit.

To think of the benefits of stretching, imagine a piece of cold chewing gum. Stretching the gum is difficult and ineffective because it is cold, stiff and inelastic. However, if you thoroughly chew the gum for a few minutes, it softens, warms up and becomes extremely pliable and you can then stretch it with ease. Your muscles are very similar. When warmed up, blood flow increases to them and they become far more elastic, permitting safer and easier movement. Your body is then working more efficiently.

With any stretching exercise, it is vital that you move into the stretched position gradually but within safe limits; only so far until you feel a slight tightness in the muscle. Once in that position, keep still, avoiding any bouncing and concentrate on a relaxed breathing pattern which will help the stretched muscle remain relaxed. No stretch should cause any form of pain; if you are experiencing pain then you have overstretched or have a damaged muscle and you should stop. Remain in this relaxed stretched position for approximately 30 seconds and than stretch the partner muscle too, so that your body remains in balance. For example, if you stretch one hamstring or one calf muscle, the other leg and hamstring or calf muscles should also be stretched to avoid developing any muscular imbalances.

A question that I am often asked is how often should you stretch? A simple answer would be as often as possible to keep thoroughly supple and loose. Practically though, just a few minutes regularly spent working on the flexibility of your major muscle groups or the particular areas that you have exercised during your workout, will reap long-term rewards in the form of a more efficient muscular system and a significantly reduced risk of muscular injury. Rather than do another weight exercise or spend a little longer on the rowing machine or swimming a few more lengths, use the time for flexibility training so that your exercise session is balanced.

By incorporating regular stretching into your routine, you will find that with a consistent programme of flexibility exercises, you're far less likely to end up with an exercise related injury – or become a 'stretcher case!'

Waiting for an injury?

The vast majority of soft tissue injuries that people suffer from are due to flexibility problems, either as a result of the repetitive nature of their activities, lifestyle generated postural problems or simply from paying insufficient attention to keeping muscles loose and supple. If you are flexible, not only are you less injury prone but you are also able to perform better because there are fewer limitations on your range of movement. You also find that because your movements are more fluid, you enjoy less tension throughout your body, which will help you remain relaxed.

So – with all these benefits from some simple stretching, what's the key? The 5 point programme below focuses upon the hows, whens and how oftens regarding stretching, so that you can add a new dimension to your training and keep those injuries at bay.

Stretching – the 5 point programme.

1. **Late is better than early**. Many people begin their training session with some stretches – usually targeting the legs. This is the wrong way to approach your training because before you do any exercise your muscles are cold and trying to stretch a cold muscle could actually result in a strain or at best, your stretch will be ineffective. A far more productive way to train is to do a progressive warm-up to supply your working muscles with blood and gradually elevate your temperature and heart rate and then take one of two paths. If your session is going to be intense, eg: fast paced running, then ensure your warm-up is lengthy and follow it with a stretching programme before you run fast. If your session is going to be less intense, eg: a recovery CV workout, then follow your short warm-up with some mobility exercises, enjoy your main session and then

stretch at the end of your workout. Note that even with a more intense workout where you may stretch earlier, don't forget to include stretching at the end as well.

2. **Breathe.** Throughout each stretch, ensure that your breathing remains relaxed. If you hold your breath (which is quite easy to do if you're straining to get into a stretched position), then you introduce tension into the body and you also risk elevating your blood pressure. This tension will limit your body's ability to stretch optimally and hence you won't maximise your flexibility training benefits.

3. **Hold for at least 30 seconds.** Stretching a muscle for just a few seconds (as you may see on television when a footballer prepares to come onto the pitch as a substitute!), brings no flexibility benefits. Instead, gradually ease into the stretch until you feel tightness in the muscle (BUT NO PAIN!) and then maintain the stretched position. Ensure that you hold the stretch for a minimum of 30 seconds because then you will find that you can actually stretch further – again, meaning that you'll get more out of your flexibility training time.

4. **Don't do anything else.** Stretching is an exercise discipline in it's own right, not an afterthought that you do whilst watching TV, or chatting to someone. Hence it is important that you put the same focus into your flexibility training as you would do when you're exercising. If you *'just go through the motions'* you'll find that you're moving your body into the correct position but not actually concentrating on maintaining the tension – which is necessary to allow the individual muscle fibres to elongate. So, focus on the task in hand, after all, a stretch takes less than a minute and you'll enjoy much better results.

5. **After every workout.** As mentioned above, the end of your workout is usually the most suitable time to stretch out and you should stretch every time you exercise because that will help your recovery and ease any post exercise stiffness the following day. It's unnecessary to attempt to stretch all the main muscles in your body because you'll find that will take much longer so instead, focus on muscles that you've specifically worked. For example: after a cycling trip, ensure you stretch out your the main muscles in your legs and any areas that you know are less flexible. Again, using the cycling example, as well as your legs, you might stretch out your chest as well (cyclists can often suffer from tightness in the chest). So, in this example, the cyclist could focus upon chest, calves, quadriceps, glutes and hamstrings – a programme which

would take less than five minutes – a very worthwhile investment of your time!

QuickTest

What's your upper body flexibility like? Try the 'Loop-the-Loop Test' and see how you fare.

1. ***Stand upright with your left arm behind your back.***
2. ***Take your right arm and reach high above your head, over your right shoulder and down your back.***
3. ***Stretch your left arm up your back and try and get your hands to meet.***
4. ***Change arms and repeat the test the opposite way.***

How did you do?

Well if you can't link your fingers or at least touch them together then your flexibility is below average. Remember that the test requires you to be able to touch your fingers together stretching alternate arms behind your back, not just the easier one!

Football

> *'Some people believe football is a matter of life and death. I'm very disappointed with that attitude. I can assure you it is much, much more important than that.'*
> **BILL SHANKLY**

Get football fit!

Football is now both a much faster and more physical game - you only have to look at pictures of the World Cup winning England team from 1966 to see how the physique of the modern footballer has changed. To play at your best, a blend of speed, strength, co-ordination and endurance is required, which coincidentally is also a pretty good mix for anyone looking to maintain a balanced fitness regime – football or not! So, with numerous teams of all ages playing matches locally each weekend, what sort of training should you be focusing upon and how often should you be working out to fit in with your matches? In addition, the following fitness components and training strategies for footballers will serve anyone who is looking to build some all-round fitness as well, so it's not just footballers that can benefit from this advice!

How to get – and stay – *football fit*

1. **Endurance training.** The continuous pace and duration of the modern game means that these days, to be successful, you have to *'have a good engine'*. How many times have you seen rival teams fold in the second half of matches, simply because their cardiovascular fitness isn't at a sufficiently high enough level to permit continuous running for 90 minutes? With match and player analysis from tools such as ProZone, it's estimated that a midfield player can cover 10K in a match – that's 6.2 miles, in a combination of sprinting and jogging – and to achieve that, you have to have good endurance. To build your basic endurance, look to complete one long run each week that builds until you can comfortably complete six miles non-stop and ideally, a second session over approximately half to two-thirds of your long run distance but run at a faster 'time-trial' pace, to help your speed endurance.

2. **Weight training.** If you want to avoid getting easily hustled off the ball then you need to build total body strength, not just in the legs. Leg strength is important for speed but working on your back, chest, arms, shoulders, and abdominals will give you more power

and control in all aspects of your game. As a start, try and factor in a minimum of one dedicated resistance training session into your programme each week and if possible, perhaps when you have fewer matches, double up to two sessions because your progression will be greater. Avoid completing a session a day or two before a match, in case you suffer from any delayed onset of muscle soreness (DOMS) which could make you feel a little stiff and sore.

3. **Core strength training.** A memorable match between Barcelona against Chelsea in the Champions League saw Ronaldinho, Barcelona's star performer, make a searing run on goal. Spotting the danger, defender John Terry sprinted in from the side in an attempt to bulldoze him off the ball but ended up completely flat on the ground himself. Ronaldinho had seen Terry's approach, momentarily paused on his run to set himself and lock in his core and Terry just bounced off him. A fantastic demonstration of the benefits of building your core strength. A few stability ball and static core strength exercises incorporated into your main resistance training programme will give that 'on-the-ball' strength that is so beneficial to helping you stay on your feet.

4. **Specific speed-work and coordination training**. If you're a member of a football club then it's likely that you will have a weekly training session covering tactics, mini-games and some basic fitness work. It is also important for these sessions to include coordination training and specific drills to give you the ability to change direction and move quickly, whilst under control. The opportunities are endless but cone-based games are effective, together with partner ball-work, which will also support other fitness training. Also, ladder and hurdle work is tremendously effective for speed, agility and quickness, so chat to your team coach if you're not already doing them!

5. **Stretching.** Yes, it's an old chestnut but how often do footballers suffer leg muscle tears and pulls? Well, if the professional brigade is anything to go by then it's very frequently! The problem with football is the explosive nature of the game and the stretching for loose balls, often under load that can cause injury. If you are inflexible then it won't stop you being competitive – you'll still want to play as you always have done but it will mean that injury is far more likely to strike, particularly as you get older. However, if you factor in some flexibility training after each session and match, you're far less likely to pick up a strain – which means that no missed matches and improved performance on the pitch.

6. **Sports massage.** A problem that professional footballers have and one which is experienced by anyone involved in regular training and competition, is recovering sufficiently in readiness for your next match or training session. One of the most effective tools in the club kitbag to promote recovery, identify any potential injury sites and prevent injury; is regular sports massage. Sports massage will flush out the waste by-products from your match or training session, re-align muscle fibres and overall, keep your muscles loose, supple and prepared for your next outing. Ideally, look to have a massage a couple of days after a match or hard session and elicit feedback from your therapist regarding any tight muscles or potential problem areas.

Getting Started

> *'A journey of a thousand miles begins with a single step.'*
>
> **CONFUCIUS**

Health and fitness focus

I recall a discussion I had with a friend whose wife didn't exercise which resulted in her struggling with her weight, strength and overall fitness. My friend lamented his wife's reluctance to get involved with exercise because he was keen for her to enjoy the health benefits that he had found from regularly working out. My reply to him was: ***'she just doesn't know how good she could feel'***. This really struck a chord and that statement perfectly encapsulates what health and fitness is all about. Health and fitness doesn't have to be about running the London Marathon, bodybuilding or taking exercise to extreme levels. It's about improving the quality of your life by exercising safely and correctly for your personal goals, combined with healthy eating, (instead of embarking on any one of the restrictive diets that are so prevalent).

So, what benefits can you expect from enjoying regular exercise?

Why should I exercise – what are the benefits?

1. **More energy.** It is something of a paradox that an activity which requires you to *expend* more energy actually results in you *having* more energy – but it's true! Regularly working out puts a spring in your stride and you find that your desire to collapse on the sofa after work diminishes because you're still full of beans!

2. **Improved quality of life.** If you don't exercise, you limit your ability to do basic activities such as any job that requires an element of strength and stamina or keeping up with your children. The 21st century is the era of stress but time out for some exercise is a proven strategy for reducing blood pressure, stress levels and the stress hormone.

3. **Reduced risk of preventable diseases.** Our modern lives are blighted by the plethora of preventable diseases that are either caused by or severely impacted by low fitness levels. Heart disease, diabetes, osteoporosis and obesity are the big hitters, yet a correctly constructed exercise programme can either keep these problems at bay or reverse the physical decline that sufferers of these conditions endure.

4. **Easier weight management.** The scourge of modern living is the nation's obsession with weight and the alarming rise in obesity levels. *'Lifestyle'* magazines espousing the merits of the latest *'I dropped 20 pounds in two weeks'* diet, frequently endorsed by a celebrity, serve only to add credence to eating plans that are doomed to failure. However, how good would it be to be able to enjoy every meal, have the occasional guilt-free indulgence and toss the calorie counting book in the bin because you neither need nor want it? Well it is possible, simply as a benefit of following a regular health and fitness routine.

5. **Looking good.** Supermodel status unfortunately eludes most of us but that doesn't mean that we don't want to look our best. Have you noticed how someone who exercises has a healthy glow, good skin tone and more colour in their face? A toned body results in clothes that fit well instead of hanging unattractively and good posture can add inches to your height and loads to your confidence. We all want to look our best and being fit *inside* is the key to looking good on the *outside*.

6. **Add life to your years.** Being fit and healthy isn't about living forever. It's about enjoying a good quality of life throughout your life, rather than succumbing to a physical decline that frequently is caused by low fitness levels. Following a regular exercise programme is a proven way of staving off so many of the problems that we assume will come our way just because we're older. Health and fitness is about improving the quality of your life today and tomorrow and maintaining that quality so that you can continue to enjoy the things that you used to be able to do when younger. As a spin-off benefit, the chance of you adding years to your life is also greatly improved – what a win!

So, with all that evidence, what are you waiting for? Well, as everyone knows, it's never quite as easy as that is it. There are several hurdles to clear in committing to getting fit, for example:

- How do I get started?
- I'm not sure how to exercise
- I'm not fit enough to work out
- I feel self conscious in the gym
- What is the best sort of exercise for me?
- I don't know if it's safe for me to exercise
- I have a medical condition that may affect my training

All these statements are valid concerns if you are unused to exercising, yet looking at the massive portfolio of benefits from starting a health and fitness programme – it's a no-brainer – exercise for life is a must for life.

Heart Health

'The heart is the body's engine and should be maintained accordingly'. ***MIKE SEARLE***

Heart disease reversed!

Each year in the UK alone, a quarter of a million people suffer a heart attack, with a third dying before they reach hospital. A pretty frightening statistic but there appears to be good news on the horizon. There has been considerable recent media interest in a revolutionary new drug that early tests in America have found can actually reverse the effects of atherosclerosis – the build-up of fatty deposits in arteries. This gradual narrowing of the arteries leads to heart attacks and strokes but the new drug can reduce these deposits by up to 9%. The drug; rosuvastatin, the newest and most potent of the statin family of cholesterol reducing drugs, reduced fatty deposits in almost 80% of the trial group and has been heralded as the 'holy grail' in the war against heart disease. Clearly this research is good news for the 2 million people in Britain who suffer from narrowing of the arteries but is it actually the Holy Grail that is being claimed in many quarters?

Anyone who is suffering from atherosclerosis is also at risk from associated problems including obesity and diabetes, so reliance on cholesterol busting medication isn't the total solution. Most people would prefer not to take medication and although statin type drugs are regarded as extremely safe, a small number of users have encountered muscle wasting problems. So to keep your heart healthy, follow the top 5 tips below, which come with many additional benefits, including feeling good, easy weight management and improved all round health!

Top 5 tips to protect your heart

1. **Get vigorous!** Studies have shown that vigorous cardiovascular exercise is more effective at keeping heart healthy than a gentle workout, so try to focus on activities such as jogging, cycling, swimming, etc; rather than lighter activities such as walking or golf.
2. **Say no to salt!** There is a proven link between salt consumption and high blood pressure, so try and reduce it as much as possible in your diet. Easy wins include eliminating it from cooking and at the table and reducing your consumption in ready made soups, convenience meals, cakes, biscuits and many 'snack-type' foods.

3. **Stub it out!** Smoking is another proven contributory factor to heart disease but quitting brings about so many other health benefits, including improved taste, appetite and complexion, let alone lowering your risk factor for a heart attack.

4. **Eat clean!** Look on the back of the packet or carton of the majority of prepared foods and you will be faced with a bewildering list of ingredients, most of which I can neither spell nor pronounce! However, a key one to look out for is Hydrogenated Fat. Hydrogenation is a process whereby food manufacturers convert a healthy fat into a far less healthy fat to serve them the purposes of increased shelf life and other manufacturing benefits. These fats are harmful to health and particularly your heart so try and avoid them at all costs.

5. **Watch your weight.** Whilst not a big advocate of focusing on weight as a measure of someone's health and fitness because body composition is a far more accurate method, as a general rule of thumb, if you are overweight then you are increasing your risk of heart disease and indeed many additional diseases, so good weight management is another tool in your heart healthy kitbag.

Get heart healthy!

So keeping your heart healthy is absolutely paramount. When you consider that coronary heart disease (the biggest killer in the country) is a preventable disease which kills more than 110,000 people in England every year with a further 1.4 million people suffering from angina and 250,000 people suffering a heart attack annually, keeping your heart healthy has to be a top priority.

So, to kick-start your heart healthy fitness programme, follow the heart-safe training tips below:

Heart-safe training tips

1. **Walk before you can run!** Start slowly and introduce your body to CV training gradually. Whatever CV exercise you take (walking, jogging, running, rowing, cycling, swimming, etc), remember that it's not just your heart that you are training. Associated muscles (particularly in the legs), tendons and even your bones have to build up in response to the new challenge, so give yourself time to adapt.

2. **Rest.** An invitation to rest might sound odd but it is absolutely key for safe, injury-free progression. Your training gains occur not

when you are actually exercising but when your body is rebuilding after your exercise sessions. Omit rest and invite injury is my maxim, so ensure that you intersperse training days with recovery days.

3. **Take a day off!** Don't be afraid to have a day off from your training. If you feel at all tired or are aching then miss a training session so that when you do exercise, you are getting a quality session.

4. **Target.** Aim to build up to and complete a minimum of five sessions lasting at least 30 minutes each time. Studies have shown that this is the minimum amount of CV exercise that will give you long lasting health benefits for your heart.

5. **Invest in a HRM.** HRM stands for Heart Rate Monitor. Historically a training tool for elite athletes, they are now available for everyone and at accessible prices. Your HRM will give you a continual readout of how hard your heart is working and display it on a special wristwatch. This works in several ways; you can monitor your performance session by session and you can check you're not exercising too hard, or not hard enough! Prices for entry level models start at around £30, which is excellent value for an ECG accurate piece of kit.

Follow these five heart-safe training tips and you are laying excellent foundations for good heart healthy cardiovascular fitness.

Holidays

> *'A change is as good as a rest'.* **ARTHUR CONAN DOYLE**

Holidays ahoy!

Once the clocks go forward, many people's thought start turning to the summer, holidays and getting in shape for the beach. Hence from springtime onwards, many people look to fast-track their fitness to get in shape for a couple of weeks '*En Vacances*'. Well unfortunately there are no quick fixes in any arena and health and fitness is no different because exercise and a healthy lifestyle needs to be an integral component of our lives – as opposed to a 'one-hit-wonder'. However, if you're looking to get *'beach fit'* and are committed to regular exercise over the coming weeks, providing that your training is correctly structured and targeted, significant results for weight loss and toning up can be achieved in a relatively short period of time.

So, what are you waiting for! Now is the time to take action and kick-start your holiday fitness regime! However, if you are serious about getting into shape for the summer then it is vital that you adhere to the following rules:

Holidays ahoy - getting in shape golden rules

1. Keep your training balanced – with something of everything
2. Include rest days in your schedule – that's when you make improvements
3. Don't neglect nutrition – it's integral to success

So assuming that you've got approximately six to eight weeks to play with before you depart, how should you tackle your training? Well, follow the six stage plan below to help you get on track, get in shape and get into that swimming costume!

Six simple steps to holiday fitness

1. **Create a plan.** If you don't know where you're going, how will you know when you've arrived? Simply saying '*I want to lose weight'* or *'I want to be fitter'* isn't enough. Instead you need to have some meaningful targets to focus upon, which could include your holiday departure date, a sensible and achievable weight loss goal and perhaps something like fitting into an item of clothing that you wore last year/two years ago – or similar. Even better is a sequence of

targets that builds towards a major target just before your holiday begins. Once you have identified your targets, write them down and then communicate them to as many people as possible because that will help to reinforce your commitment.

2. **Make time.** Now that you've identified your destination, you need to commit sufficient time to make your journey successful. If one of your goals is to sensibly lose three quarters of a stone through smart eating and regular exercise then you need to find time for that exercise. A useful strategy is to involve your family in your plans so that everyone buys into what you're trying to achieve. For example, household chores can be shared around and then 'time for you' becomes a little easier to find.

3. **Burn up those calories!** If weight loss is one of your goals then part of your training needs to be focused upon burning calories. Calorie burning can take many different forms, for example walking to and from work, specific cardiovascular exercise such as cycling, jogging, exercise classes, gym training, etc and overall, seeking out ways to be more active throughout the day. In addition, don't neglect training with weights because lifting weights builds muscle and muscle burns calories 24 hours a day, even when you're not exercising. In case anyone is concerned about turning into Arnold Schwazenegger then worry not! Women won't turn into muscle-bound bodybuilders – in fact far from it. What you can achieve is a toned body that fits into your clothes without bulges in the wrong places.

4. **Nutrition is key.** An integral part of your healthy lifestyle changes is to look at your current nutrition and target some easy wins. For example, swapping lower calorie foods for high calorie ones, such as a slice of toast instead of a couple of croissants for breakfast, fruit instead of biscuits and water for sugar laden drinks. Also look for simple swaps such as reducing your alcohol intake (because alcohol is dead calories) and large quantities of butter on bread and sandwiches.

5. **CV alone isn't enough!** Even if you're unused to the weights and mats area of the gym, it's important that you venture in there regularly. Without any resistance training, whilst you may lose some weight, you'll not achieve that toned look and build all important strength so you need to support your CV (cardiovascular training) with a total body resistance training programme. The benefits will be to tone up all over, improve your posture and burn calories. Remember to keep your workout completely balanced and correctly tailored for you, your current fitness levels and goals

and seek professional support to ensure that you train safely, correctly and maximise your training time with suitable exercises.

6. **Have a reward!** To help you maintain your focus once the first flush of enthusiasm has dissipated a little, when you reach one of your mini targets en route to your primary goal, give yourself a reward. I'm not suggesting that you go for a major blowout and undo all the good work from the previous weeks; that would be pointless. Instead, treat yourself to something longer lasting, perhaps some new clothes, some modern exercise kit – or whatever is a suitable reward to you. Tick off your progress on your plan and then refocus upon your next target as you move towards your goal.

Holiday maintenance fitness

When the school summer holidays are upon us, most people will be taking some time out with their families for a break and leaving the term-time and 9 to 5 routine behind for a while. Whilst everyone eagerly anticipates a break, of course this also means that it's quite likely that regular exercise is also put on hold. A short break from training can be beneficial because it allows the body time to rest and recuperate but as many people can testify, once you're out of your exercise routine, it can be difficult to re-motivate yourself to get started again. This problem can be compounded with the length of the school holiday period and also the possibility that the combined effects of less exercise and *'a few holiday excesses'*, can result not only in reduced fitness but also unwanted weight gain when September comes around. Now whilst I'm not advocating a rigid, structured and intensive training programme whilst you're enjoying your holiday, it does make sense to at least keep your fitness ticking over during the summer, not least so that you don't lose those hard-earned gains from earlier in the year.

So below are ideas and suggestions to help you maintain your fitness whilst the schools are out and then September won't be a time of dread!

Tips and ideas to stay fit on holiday.

1. **Rest up!** Firstly, it's important to emphasise that your holiday should be about having a holiday rather than rigidly adhering to a strict regime – unless of course your holiday is a specific training camp type holiday centred around your chosen sport. However, assuming that your break is more conventional then it's key to back off on the volume and intensity of your usual training because not only will you return physically invigorated, you'll also return

mentally refreshed and then you'll be raring to go again. It's only if you shut down completely, perhaps for several weeks that you'll lose fitness and probably regret your extended period of rest.

2. **Make a maintenance commitment!** As with so many things, if you don't plan ahead and have a goal, it is much harder to factor in fitness into your life – let alone during your holiday or the six weeks until September! So, if you make a conscious decision to stay in shape over the summer then you're much more likely to achieve your goal. Even better, your goal doesn't have to be overly challenging, such as losing a set amount of weight, or running further or faster, all you need to commit to is maintenance fitness – so that you can resume in the autumn where you left off this month.

3. **Divide by two!** A useful rule of thumb to help you maintain fitness is to use a *'divide by two'* rule. For example, if you usually enjoy exercising four times a week – ie: typically every other day then cut it down to just a couple of sessions. The idea is to keep your fitness levels ticking over rather than extending yourself. You can apply the divide by two rule to however many weekly exercise sessions that you usually do or alternatively, factor in some sort of exercise every other day.

4. **Go easy!** Still in keeping with the easier theme, don't forget to reduce the intensity of your workouts as well. For cardiovascular training sessions, opt for some steady-paced training rather than fast, hard and intense workouts. Similarly, if you usually lift weights in the gym then rather than pushing on each exercise, try reducing the sets and/or repetitions that you would normally complete and reducing the weight on some elements of your usual programme. You won't lose fitness or strength because you're still completing a beneficial workout but in line with the recuperation theme, you'll allow your body to recharge its batteries. Studies have shown that if you work out at a lower intensity than your usual session, ie: a maintenance workout, then your fitness losses over 10-14 days will be low.

5. **Incorporate fitness into your day!** Any parent who has spent several hours on the beach digging holes and building sandcastles will know they've worked their muscles; if not at the time then certainly the following day! So a useful strategy to keep your fitness ticking over is to include exercise with your holiday activities. As well as beach based activities which could also include races, games of cricket or rounders, etc, snorkelling, swimming, walking or perhaps a family cycle ride are all useful

adjuncts to your usual routine and as well as keeping your fitness levels ticking over, will build up a healthy appetite for the evening!

6. **Watch those extras!** How often has someone said to you: *'I only have to look at a cake/bar of chocolate and I put on half a stone'.* Now whilst I'm not suggesting that your vacation should be a time for complete abstinence and a monk-like existence, it makes sense to keep a weather eye on extra calories. Generous breakfasts, alcohol in larger and more frequent quantities, laden desserts and less activity could all conspire to leave you undoing the good work that you've achieved through the year so remember to keep everything in balance and watch yourself on those 'all you can eat buffets!'

7. **Exercise late or early.** Whether you're heading away to warmer and sunnier climes or just enjoying a family break, fitting in some exercise either first thing in the morning or after the day's activities is ideal. A quick session at the beginning or end of the day doesn't interfere with everyone else's holiday and if the weather is hot, exercising at this time avoids trying to complete a workout in uncomfortably hot conditions.

8. **When you get home . . .** Your next challenge on returning home after your holiday is to 'get back into the saddle' and get back into training. Of course you're still likely to be 'in holiday mode' and it won't be long before work rears it's head so similarly, make a commitment to keep your routine going. Even if you simply continue your maintenance programme whilst you readjust, you're unlikely to lose a great deal of fitness – which after all is the key during the summer period.

SuperTip

If you're worried about losing muscle strength because you'll be reducing your training over the next few weeks, make sure that when you do exercise, you train at the same intensity as usual. Studies have found that if you have to reduce your usual training but complete workouts at the same intensity every 10 days, you won't progress your fitness but you'll certainly minimise your losses.

Home Exercise

> *'We shall never have any more time. We have and always have had, all the time there is'.* **ARNOLD BENNETT**

Home help

For many people, it can be a real challenge finding the time to fit exercise into the day, let alone the extra time needed to travel to a gym or Health Club – which can often mean that your exercise routine gets left on the shelf. Yes, everyone is aware that they should exercise regularly but by the time you've packed your kitbag, travelled to and from the gym and all the other little things that frequently happen whilst you're there; a gym visit can seriously impact on your available time. However there is a simple, accessible and effective solution and that's to exercise at home. Modern gyms have a fantastic array of specialist exercise equipment and are the ideal location to get the absolute maximum benefits from your workout but what if you simply can't make it? Well, with a little ingenuity, you can enjoy a CV, flexibility, core and resistance training workout in the comfort of or the vicinity of your own home and save time into the bargain, so no gym doesn't have to mean no exercise!

To get you thinking, look at the following practical ideas to help you work out at or from home, so that irrespective of your schedule, your fitness doesn't have to suffer.

Home help exercise ideas and benefits.

- **Stage 1: Go shopping!** For a modest outlay you can buy a small set of dumbbells, an exercise mat, a stability ball and pump and if you need to, suitable trainers. Whilst you can always compromise with basic items of clothing to work out in, with footwear you can't because correct training shoes are a valuable investment in comfort, support and injury prevention.

- **Stage 2: Find your space!** For your indoor sessions, you need to earmark a room or somewhere where you have enough space to stretch out and carry out a wide variety of exercises. All you need is somewhere that is a minimum of two metres square – your lounge could be ideal.

- **Stage 3: Get planning!** Begin by planning in just two sessions per week. Session one will focus on your CV training + flexibility and the second session will also focus on flexibility, together with core and strength training. Identify when the best times will be for your workouts and telegraph that to everyone else so that you can factor in quality, uninterrupted time for you.

- **Stage 4: CV training.** For your CV exercise, you don't need your indoor space because the simplest and most time effective solution is to exercise outside. One of the great benefits of outdoor training is that you don't need any specialist equipment. Walking, jogging, running and cycling are all excellent forms of CV exercise that you can carry out directly out of your own front door. Start slowly and build up gradually and always start and finish your session with a minimum of five minutes gentle warming up, which will help prepare your body for your main session and also enhance your performance. CV exercise is the most important element of your training simply because it helps ensure that that your heart remains in good shape.

- **Stage 5: Resistance training.** Using your indoor workout space, a combination of exercises using your own bodyweight, your dumbbell set and your stability ball can give you a total body and core workout. Your choice of exercises is key and you should always focus on following correct technique during every movement so that you both enjoy maximum fitness gains and also avoid injury. Working out with weights will build and maintain strength all around your body and has never been more important than in the 21st century where our computer, car and labour saving lives have severely impacted on our muscular strength and consequent health and fitness.

- **Stage 6: Flexibility training.** This one's very easy to factor in because flexibility training doesn't require any additional sessions – all you have to do is to include five minutes stretching at the end of each of your two workouts. After your CV session, focus upon leg stretching because your legs muscles are used for all your CV workouts. For your resistance training sessions, focus upon the muscle groups of the upper body. To select which muscles to target, pick ones where you found the exercise more challenging because that will help ease any post exercise soreness that you may experience the following day. Regular stretching keeps you loose and supple and is a vital part of injury prevention.

Injury

'The majority of soft tissue injuries are a result of incorrect training protocols'. ***MIKE SEARLE***

Oh no – I'm injured!

A lot of people believe and accept that injuries are a necessary by-product of their training with the misconception that 'you just have to put up with them'. Many people train through injuries, carry injuries, or simply put up with pain and discomfort, reduced muscle function or periods of training downtime because they assume that there is no other option. Well my ethos is different, injuries should not be part and parcel of your sport, in fact they should be completely the opposite; unusual occurrences.

An injury slows you down, prevents you training or competing, makes you less functional and causes undue pain and frustration. The old adage, prevention is better than cure is entirely applicable to injuries and by following some simple, basic protocols, you have a much better chance of continuing with your chosen activity week in, week out. The key causes of injuries are:

1. **Too much, too soon.** By increasing your training load too quickly, you are not allowing your body sufficient time to adapt to the new stresses that you are placing it under. Always aim to progress gradually, so that you avoid fatigue, illness and of course injury.

2. **Too little recovery.** Improvements in your training do not occur during the training session itself but in the rest periods when you are not training. When you are resting, your body is adapting and rebuilding itself stronger so that subsequent training sessions become easier. Omit recovery days and you are heading down the road towards breakdown.

3. **Insufficient supplementary training.** Often, people limit their exercise to a single activity, for example, solely running or solely weight-training. This invariably results in imbalances in the body because a total body workout is not being followed. Eventually, these imbalances will result in muscle strains or other injuries. For optimum all-round health and fitness, we should aim to exercise the cardiovascular system (heart and lungs), muscles and also include core and flexibility training.

4. **Incorrect footwear.** There are a huge range of training shoes on the market, for every conceivable activity and gait. However, with such a vast selection available, it is easy to make an unsuitable choice because everyone has different requirements. For any sort of impact activity, such as aerobics, running, etc, an incorrect shoe is very likely to result in an injury and so it is worthwhile seeking out a specialist retailer who can provide advice on the best footwear solution for you and the exercise that you do.

5. **Insufficient flexibility.** Lack of flexibility accounts for a very high proportion of injuries. Tight, inflexible muscles are far more likely to succumb to injury because of their reduced range of movement and functionality. The solution is to follow a programme of regular stretching, which will help keep your muscles pliable and loose, so that you don't 'pull' muscles when exercising.

6. **Competition.** Competition places additional stresses and strains on the body because your competitive instincts take over, the adrenaline flows, you strive towards a long-held goal, or you race against a rival. A single competitive outing can cause injury if you have not fully warmed up or you are under-prepared for the competition when you are subjecting your body to greater loads. The answer is not to compete too frequently, allow adequate recovery between competitions and employ sports massage and developmental flexibility to ward off injury. This way you are giving your muscles the best chance of recovery before their next exertion.

SuperTip

If you are unfortunate enough to get injured, your training downtime isn't entirely wasted. Whilst you are undergoing treatment and rehabilitation, spend some time evaluating your exercise programme to find out how and why you have suffered an injury. By seeking advice on how to adapt your post-injury training, you can safeguard against the injury recurring and when you return to exercise, you are far less likely to suffer injury downtime again!

First Aid for injuries

With soft tissue injuries (eg: muscle and tendon strains) being so common amongst people who exercise, flexibility training will go a long way to help you stay injury free. However, there may still be times when you are unfortunate enough to get injured; possibly through a contact sport such as football or perhaps because you have overstepped the mark with your training.

So, if you do suffer from an injury, what should you do to manage it and what steps can you take to help your recovery so that you can return to your favourite activities as soon as possible?

The first thing that you should do on suffering an injury is to act FAST! The quicker you act the better so that you help the healing process. Your immediate post-injury actions should follow the acronym **PRICE**, which stands for:

1. **P = Protect.** The injured limb or part of the body should be protected from further trauma. If necessary, you should immobilise the area so that it is impossible to use it. If you fail to fully protect the injury, it is possible that you will make it worse through additional movement.

2. **R = Rest.** By resting the area, you are helping to reduce blood flow and tissue fluids to the injury site, which in turn will help reduce swelling and inflammation. Typically, this period will be for 24 to 48 hours.

3. **I = Ice.** Applying an ice pack to the injury will further help to reduce swelling and inflammation and if the injury is painful, will also provide a degree of pain relief. For a quick and easy DIY icepack, keep a pack of frozen peas handy in the freezer. If you need to apply ice to an injury, simply wrap the pack in a tea-towel and apply to the injury as frequently as possible during the first 24 hours. Always follow a '5 minutes on, 10 minutes off' protocol to avoid damaging your skin.

4. **C = Compress.** Compressing the icepack around the injured muscle is another strategy to help reduce swelling because compression reduces the available space for swelling to occur.

5. **E = Elevate.** Finally, by elevating the injured limb, for example, you could put your foot up on a stool; you help prevent a build-up of fluid around the injury site.

Depending on the nature and severity of your injury, after a period of between 24 to 72 hours, you need to start rehabilitation. Your rehab should follow a structured programme that is designed to gradually rehabilitate you back to full strength, flexibility, functionality and fitness.

The protocols to follow are:

1. **Flexibility training.** Inflexible muscles and tendons are a prime cause of injuries and repeat injuries and following a correctly prescribed Flexibility Programme is a key component of your recovery. It is important that the injured muscle is stretched carefully and progressively so that your post-injury range of movement is not compromised.

2. **Massage.** Sports Massage is a powerful tool that will help drain excess fluid from within the damaged tissues, flush waste products away, align the repairing muscle fibres and increase the overall pliability or elasticity of the muscle. Without employing massage therapy, frequently, the muscle fibres do not completely align, resulting in a weakened structure that is subsequently more prone to injury.

3. **Ultrasound.** Another powerful tool, which can often be used on an injury where more invasive treatments such as Sports Massage would cause discomfort. Applied correctly, Ultrasound can penetrate deep into a repairing muscle and is effective at pain reduction, breaking up scar tissue and promoting healing.

4. **Strength and mobility training.** This phase of your rehab should be closely monitored with gradual increases in intensity as the injury repairs. Initially, it may be necessary to do very light assisted movements with no resistance, followed by self-movement and eventually movements against resistance. As your condition improves, sport or activity specific training can commence, progressively working towards previous levels of volume and intensity and finally, a return to full activity.

SuperTip

When rehabilitating from injury, your end goal should not be a return to previous levels of fitness. Instead, your target should be to return stronger and more flexible. In this way, the weaknesses that resulted in the injury occurring are negated and you will be safeguarding yourself from a repeat injury to the same area.

London Marathon

'I'm not really a marathon man'.
STEVE JONES, FORMER MARATHON WORLD RECORD HOLDER

YOU CAN run the London Marathon!

Who would have thought when the late Chris Brasher dreamed up the concept of a mass participation marathon, that arguably the toughest event in the athletics calendar would prove so popular from elite athletes to octogenarians alike. He called the marathon 'the suburban Everest', which is an extremely fitting description. Since the inaugural race back in 1981, over 700,000 runners have successfully completed the 26.2 mile course from Greenwich to Westminster and raised hundreds of millions of pounds for charity in the process.

Over 30,000 runners annually complete the classic course, finishing on the Queen's doorstep outside Buckingham Palace in The Mall, which is both a sight to behold and an amazing experience. The crowd support is fantastic with Londoners out in their tens of thousands to voice their support for every runner and hanging off any available vantage point all around the route. At times you feel like you're running through a wall of sound, so loud is their cheering and by the finish line you feel almost deafened!

If you've watched the race on television and looked on in admiration as so many ordinary men and women achieve their dream, I can assure you that to experience it all at first hand is incredible. I cannot convey in words the excitement and magnitude of the whole experience and I wholeheartedly recommend it to anyone, whatever your age or current level of fitness. Furthermore, with correct training, you too can run the London Marathon and if you feel sufficiently enthused to take up the challenge, entry forms are available in the summer from sports shops. If you would like to run the marathon, it's never too early to start training because the earlier you start, the better chance you are giving yourself of building up steadily and allowing your body enough time to adjust to the new demands that you are placing upon it. Additionally, it is important that you follow a structured training programme that is correct for you and seeking professional advice is invaluable to ensure that your training is correctly planned and can take you to where you want to go, safely and effectively.

So, could you take up the challenge of the London Marathon? The answer must be a definite yes; after all, a 94 year old runner has completed the race; so why not you? Running a marathon, has to be one of life's great achievements so why not think about improving your fitness and entering the race? Yes the training takes time and no, the marathon isn't easy but then if it was, there would be no sense of achievement on completing it.

SuperTip

As a rule of thumb, when you are three weeks away from Marathon race day, your weekly mileage should decrease by 25% each week. This enables your body to recover from the continuous training and rebuild stronger so that you will be in the best possible shape when it matters. You are then giving yourself the best possible chance to arrive on the start line refreshed.

London countdown

When it's just one week before race day, all prospective London Marathoners should be well into their tapering programme, easing back on both the volume and the intensity of their training as their date in the capital approaches. To ensure that you enjoy the big day, there are several things that you can do (and also many things that you should not do!) that can make a huge difference to your race experience. Key point number one is planning. Over the final week, you will enjoy more free time because your training volume has reduced. This additional time is an excellent opportunity to finalise all your arrangements to help ensure that everything runs smoothly, so follow these top six tapering tips to help with your preparation:

London Marathon top five tapering tips

1. **Nutrition is key.** To correctly fuel your body to run 26.2 miles, you need to store as much carbohydrate as possible. This means that in the final days before the race, you need to concentrate on regular high carbohydrate meals and avoid feeling low on energy at any time. Pasta and rice are top of the charts for the sorts of food that you should be eating. Make sure that you don't leave your carbohydrate loading until Saturday at the race Pasta Party because it can take several days for the body to completely restock your fuel tanks so keep topped up throughout the week.

2. **Hydrate.** Keeping your fluid levels high is also extremely important. You're going to be exercising for several hours and although there are plenty of drinks stations around the course, it is vital to arrive at the start line completely hydrated. Even a small percentage loss of fluid can impair your performance so give yourself the best chance of success and line up at Blackheath topped up. That means focusing on drinking water throughout the week and avoiding or reducing your intake of drinks such as tea, coffee, colas and of course alcohol, which all dehydrate you.

3. **Relax, relax, relax.** Whatever your level of fitness, completing 26.2 miles under your own steam is a significant achievement. The marathon requires a huge effort so you need to take things as easy as possible during the final week and mentally prepare yourself for the challenge ahead. By setting aside some quality relaxation time where you can really chill out far from the madding crowds, you will be able to focus your mind on the task ahead, which will improve your performance on race day.

4. **Look sharp!** As you wind your training down before the big push, it is important not to slow down and become sluggish. When you arrive on the start line, you want to feel fresh, full of energy and champing at the bit for the starting pistol to fire. To avoid feelings of sluggishness, you need to maintain some quality in your training. During your final few short runs next week, inject a few short bursts of pace to keep everything 'fired up'. That doesn't mean flat out sprints or time-trials - that would be too intense. Instead, try increasing your pace to approximately 75% of your maximum speed for 80 metres, followed by a very easy jog, five times during each of your last few easy runs. Afterwards, you should feel energised and zippy, not tired.

5. **Kit yourself out.** Your choice of kit to wear on race day should be quite simple because you should wear kit that you've tried, tested and worn in. A 26.2 mile footrace is not the time to experiment with a new running top or a brand new pair of shoes. Any chafing problems which you could address over shorter training runs at home will become magnified in the marathon and could cause discomfort. The key point to remember is to choose garments that are comfortable because you'll be out on the streets of London for several hours.

Medical Conditions

> *'By making ourselves fitter, stronger and more independent, we are making ourselves better members of the human race'.*
>
> ***Bruce Tulloh, European 5000 Metres Gold Medallist***

Good health!

Just because you suffer from a medical problem doesn't necessarily rule you out from taking exercise. Any medical condition will have specific precautions and protocols that you need to be aware of when you are exercising but if you suffer from diabetes, asthma, hypertension and many other disorders, you can still get involved in carefully structured exercise that will improve your health and often, your medical condition too.

Always approach your Doctor if you plan to change your lifestyle and take more exercise, start slowly and exercise within your own limitations. Remember, your exercise programme is specifically for you and no-one else, you're not in competition and the benefits that you'll enjoy are exclusively yours. So, to help you get started, listed below are some of the most common medical conditions, together with some tips and precautions to make sure that your training is safe.

Common medical conditions and their exercise precautions.

1. **Diabetes.** Characterised by an inability to regulate blood sugar levels or produce insulin (the hormone that controls the levels of glucose in the bloodstream), diabetes affects 1.5 million people in the UK. Sufferers should be cautious of impact activities in case of damage to the feet and also be conscious of the timing of their exercise sessions in line with food intake. Benefits include better weight control, less reliance on medication and a lower risk of heart disease.

2. **Asthma.** A respiratory disease where the airways are restricted, resulting in breathlessness and difficulty in breathing; there are approximately 5 million asthma sufferers in the UK. If you suffer from asthma, try to avoid exercising in either cold or dusty environments, monitor your peak flow reading closely and ensure that your warm-up is extended. Regular CV exercise will improve lung capacity and your efficiency at utilising oxygen and hence the frequency of asthma attacks.

3. **Hypertension.** High blood pressure affects approximately 10 million people in the UK and is a proven risk factor for many conditions including heart and kidney disease and strokes. If you suffer from hypertension, avoid lifting weights overhead and ensure that your CV exercise is carried out at a careful and controlled level. Benefits include reduced blood pressure and an overall improvement in the quality of your life.
4. **Osteoporosis.** Brittle bone disease will affect approximately 33% of all women and 9% of men at some time during their lifetime, and there are currently approximately 7 million sufferers in the UK. Weight bearing activities will help increase bone density but high impact exercise which could result in fractures should be avoided. By maintaining muscular strength and bone density through exercise, the risk of fractures at the most common fracture sites (hip and wrist) is reduced.
5. **Arthritis.** With an estimated 8 million UK sufferers, arthritis has many variants but typically results in painful and inflamed joints. If you suffer from one of the forms of arthritis, exercise will help maintain your strength, mobility and posture but should be carefully monitored and controlled in line with your condition. By maintaining as much fitness as possible, you will be able to carry out everyday tasks easier and for longer.

Va va voom your asthma!

Asthma, the respiratory disease that causes narrowing of the airways and breathing problems, is becoming more prevalent amongst both children and adults. Current estimates are that in excess of 5 million people are affected in the UK alone and the sight of someone using an inhaler is increasingly common. An asthma attack can be extremely frightening as sufferers struggle to get sufficient air and hence it is no great surprise that asthmatics often avoid exercise because of the breathless feelings that exercise can generate.

However, the irony is that a carefully structured and monitored exercise programme can bring numerous benefits to an asthmatic in many ways, including:

Super-six benefits of exercise for asthmatics

1. Exercise improves your muscular strength and endurance.
2. As you get fitter, you become more efficient at utilising oxygen – so less breathless.
3. You become less sensitive to dyspnoea or shortness of breath.
4. Exercise Induced Asthma symptoms are reduced.

5. Your airways become less sensitive so you suffer fewer asthma attacks.
6. Your need for asthma medication reduces.

There are many examples of asthmatics who have reached the very pinnacle of their sports, including Marathon World Record Holder Paula Radcliffe and footballer Paul Scholes, despite their condition.

So if you're a sufferer, what steps can you take to get fit, stay fit and importantly, help your condition and improve the quality of your life?

Top Ten Tips for exercise with asthma

1. **GP check-up.** Before you embark on an exercise programme, discuss your plans with your Doctor. Your GP will welcome your intentions and will be able to further advise you on exercise precautions.

2. **Think safety.** For safety reasons and as a psychological boost, keep your inhaler close at hand during your workout. This is particularly important at the start of your programme when your body is gearing up to the new challenge of exercise.

3. **Peak early!** Monitor your Peak Flow both daily and before exercise, ensuring that you only train if your reading is at 80% or better of your personal best score.

4. **Go aerobic!** Controlled cardiovascular exercise will dramatically improve your aerobic system. Focus on aerobic training more than weight-training exercises.

5. **Warm-up well**. Always begin with a very thorough warm-up – 10 to 15 minutes is suitable.

6. **Choose your exercise.** Any exercise that gets your heart and lungs working will be beneficial, so walking, jogging, running, rowing, cycling and gym machines are all good. Also think about swimming because the damp atmosphere is helpful and also, your horizontal position in the water can help clear mucus.

7. **Cool-down, cool-down.** Always finish your exercise session with an extended cool-down, similar to your warm-up, which will help ensure that bronchospasm (narrowing of the airways) doesn't occur.

8. **Lighten the load.** For your resistance training workouts, choose lighter weights and higher repetitions instead of heavy weights.

9. **Warm and wet.** Avoid exercising in dusty, dry or cold conditions; they're far more likely to aggravate your condition.

10. **Avoid stress.** Stress can be an asthma trigger factor and can also exacerbate the symptoms of an attack. Try and keep your exercise session relaxed (and enjoyable!) and also try and limit stress in general.

SuperTip

Some research has suggested that a high intake of salt can restrict airways and reduce airflow in the lungs but at the moment the evidence is inconclusive. However, there is a proven link between a high salt intake and high blood pressure so whether it helps your asthma or not, slashing the salt is a sound strategy!

Asthma is not a total barrier to exercise and in fact exercise can actually help the condition and if you follow the Top Ten Tips above, not only can your asthma symptoms reduce but you will also enjoy a whole host of exercise benefits including easier weight management, better all-round health, more energy and more va va voom!

Under pressure!

High Blood Pressure (BP) or Hypertension, is endemic in the UK with approximately 16 million sufferers; an enormous percentage of the adult population. Currently, 60% of strokes are caused by high BP and as any GP will tell you, prevention is better than cure and the best strategy is to take steps to keep your cardiovascular system healthy – and hence avoid the need to take prescribed medication.

There are many positive steps that you can take to help keep your BP at healthy levels so let's look at five straightforward strategies to help keep yours within safe limits.

Blood pressure busting Tips

1. **Exercise for England!** Yes, it's an old chestnut – but it's so true and it works so well that it has to be the No. 1 tip. Aerobic exercise is extremely effective at lowering or staving off high BP and studies have shown that aerobic training can lower your BP by as much as 10 points *(American College of Sports Medicine, 1997)*. Any controlled activity such as walking, jogging, swimming, cycling etc that raises your heart rate and gets you slightly breathless is suitable, carried out several times a week for at least 20 minutes at a time.

2. No stress! Now this is a difficult one because modern-day fast paced living can be extremely stressful with endless deadlines and pressure. However in addition to exercise, there are simple strategies that you can employ that will give you a time-out from stressful periods, including:

    a. Putting your stressful situation in proper perspective, eg: how much does it really matter if you're 3 minutes late.
    b. Sharing a problem with a trusted friend.
    c. Time for you, away from work and other commitments
    d. Avoiding overwork.
    e. Having alcohol free days.
    f. Limiting you caffeine intake from tea, coffee and cola drinks.

3. **No salt!** Salt, 'the silent killer' is a known contributor to high BP and is a simple factor to tackle in your war against potential hypertension. Try not to add salt to your cooking, or at the table, in fact if you can banish it from your home completely, you are making a really positive change. Also, check out food labels for products that are high in salt. Ones to monitor are tinned soups, sauces, ready meals, biscuits, tinned meats, in fact the majority of processed foods. Reducing the level of salt in your diet is guaranteed to lower your blood pressure – another useful weapon in your armoury.

4. **Give up!** Give up smoking because smoking is another contributor to high BP. Not an easy one to tackle, particularly if you have smoked for many years but the consequences of not giving up are far more serious.

5. **Maintain a healthy weight.** Being overweight is becoming a very serious problem in this country because it is the precursor to a multitude of health problems, not least of which is high BP. I am

generally against the current 'over focus' on pure weight loss over the importance of leading a healthy lifestyle that embraces healthy eating and sensible exercise but when weight becomes such a factor that your health is affected then losing weight (or more accurately body fat) has to be a primary objective.

SuperTip

What does my Blood Pressure reading mean?

Blood Pressure readings are always quoted as two figures, one over the other, as in 120 over 65. (120/65). The upper figure (120) is the systolic pressure, when your heart pumps out. The lower figure (65) is the diastolic pressure, a measure of the resistance when your heart is relaxed. As a rule of thumb, if your BP is 140/90 or less, you're doing just fine!

Beware the C-word

Cancer is a huge problem and with approximately 300,000 people newly diagnosed annually, there is still much work to be done to eradicate it. Leading cancer charity Cancer Research UK has identified that there is now an increase in obesity related cancers and if you're overweight, your risk of developing breast, womb, prostate, gall bladder, kidney, colon and pancreatic cancers is greater because being overweight upsets the environment for cells and also the fat secreting hormones that can trigger tumours. Additional findings identified that slim adults in the 21st century are pretty much as slim as their counterparts ten years ago but the difference is with overweight people, where the heaviest people are now much heavier than they were ten years ago. This is supported by separate statistics that found that between 1994 and 2004, the number of obese adults rose to nearly 25% of the population – a figure that is highly likely to have increased since the study.

Now as consumers, we are in complete control of cutting our risk of these preventable diseases, ie: overweight related cancers, so below are a plethora of tips to help you slash your chances of becoming a cancer statistic and also to improve your overall health and fitness into the bargain.

Stay slim, stay healthy – 8 easy calorie reduction tips

1. **How big is your plate?** Have you ever been to the USA? Well if you have, you're bound to have noticed their massive portion sizes and 'all you can eat buffets' that leave even the best UK trenchermen struggling. Portion control is key here – it shouldn't be perceived as an insult to leave something on your plate.

2. **High calorie = low health.** You may not feel that you're eating large meals or even eating that often but if your food choices are incorrect then weight management becomes hard. Nowadays, with the popularity of convenience foods, overdosing on high calorie foods is easy and many foods contain 'hidden or empty' calories that contribute little to your nutrition but lots to your waistline.

3. **Watch those drinks.** No, not alcohol because soft drinks can be just as deadly. A standard can of Coca Cola contains approximately ten (yes ten!!) teaspoons of sugar and if you try that in your tea next time you brew up you'll get the picture! And all that sugar is yet another example of empty calories. Switch to water or squash and feel the difference!

4. **Coffee to go?** There has been a huge rise in the number of takeaway coffee shops on the high street and these days it is common to see people sipping from a carton en route to work. However, spare a thought for how many calories are in your large double chocolate mocha with whipped cream and syrup. A couple of big hitters like that each day and you could be consuming approximately half of your daily calorie requirements just in your coffee-break – and that's not counting any meals! So, rein in those speciality drinks and you'll rein in excess calories too.

5. **What's your poison?** Yes, alcohol is a poison - albeit one that does actually bring some health benefits when you consume it in small doses. However, it is also calorie consumption that's an easy win if you're looking to lose weight. For example, a pint of beer ranges from a couple of hundred calories to close to 600 calories per pint and if as a male, you typically require around 2,500 calories per day, it's easy to see how a few nights out can leave you with an expanding waistline. Consider lower strength drinks and alternating alcohol with sparkling water – your head will thank you for it in the morning!

6. **Keep regular.** When is temptation time for you? Chances are it's mid afternoon when you get 'the munchies' and are tempted to reach for a chocolate bar, handful of biscuits, or similar high

calorie, low nutritional snack. Often the culprit here is irregularity with mealtimes, possibly a missed lunch, or a quick bite in the car between appointments, with the end result that later in the afternoon your blood sugar dips and your brain receives signals saying – 'I'm hungry'. What then could be easier – or more attractive than a quick chocolate covered snack? However, if you can eat sensible and regular meals, temptation disappears and so do those unhelpful calories.

7. **Eat like a King.** Well actually, breakfast like a King. Many people miss breakfast, citing that they're too busy and they'll grab a snack mid-morning to keep them going – which they probably do. However, having fasted all night, by the time they get their snack, it could be up to 16 hours since any fuel has passed their lips and you know what – those calorie dense, low nutrition foods just hit the spot – temporarily. If any of that scenario sounds at all familiar, the solution is to have breakfast – cereal only takes a minute to prepare and you'll begin your day with a full fuel tank – with much less likelihood of visiting the demon vending machine at 1030!

8. **Gimme five!** Yes, we've all heard of the 5-a-day drive; to eat a minimum of five portions of fruit and vegetables per day but you know it's not just for the vitamins, minerals and 'au natural' nutritional benefits that you enjoy from eating fresh produce. Fruit and vegetables are packed with fibre, which slows down the release of energy in your digestive system, which means that you remain fuelled up for longer and feel full as well.

If you really want to turbo-charge your weight loss and rev up your metabolic engine so that you burn more calories day-in, day-out, then hit the exercise trail. Not one of the previous tips mentioned exercise but if you're serious about keeping healthy and getting the most out of your life then whilst correct nutrition is definitely on the menu, exercise is more than simply an aperitif.

Motivation & Inspiration

'Where there's a will, there's a way'. **ENGLISH PROVERB**

Motivate and rejuvenate!

One of the more common exercise problems that people struggle with is motivation. Motivation is a key component of your training because it gets you out of the door, it keeps you going when you're tired and for performance purposes, it can mean the difference between success and failure. You only have to look at the faces of the thousands of runners approaching the finish line in the London Marathon to see personal motivations etched into their features. Motivation is extremely important to achieving real benefits from your health and fitness programme and motivational strategies will help you keep going when the going gets tough.

Top motivational strategies

1. **Help someone else.** It's amazing how the incentive of helping someone else can keep you training and spur you onto great things. For example, many thousands of runners who complete the London Marathon are raising much needed cash for charity and when their bodies are saying 'no more', they are able to focus on sponsorship figures and the knowledge that if they can complete the race, they'll be helping someone who is less fortunate than themselves. Without that focus point, pounding the streets through the worst that winter throws at us in order to be fit for 26.2 miles in April can be extremely challenging but because someone else is in the equation, you're motivated to keep going.

2. **Look good!** To a greater or lesser degree, we all want to look our best – it's only natural and of course to keep your body in shape year in, year out, you've got to work at it and hence looking good is an excellent motivator to following a regular exercise programme. As well as enjoying health benefits, most people also enjoy feeling that they are in shape and are making the most of what they've got, so if that's a motivator for you, a combination of CV sessions and resistance training each week will help you achieve that goal.

3. **Pound those pounds!** With weight management an increasing problem in the developed world, either losing weight or avoiding weight gain is a key motivator for many people. If you'd like to lose

weight, don't attempt a body blitzing diet and don't expect an overnight sensation but do set yourself a realistic target. Perhaps shedding a stone within three months, which equates to losing a little over a pound a week, could motivate you. If that seems too little and too far away, remember that a losing a stone means burning off over 50,000 calories, or approximately 250 pints of beer, so if you're up for a challenge. . !

4. **Live longer!** It's a fact. Following a regular exercise programme protects against numerous preventable diseases and also lowers the incidence of many others. For example, statistics from the NHS have shown that exchanging cigarettes for a gym membership to get fit could increase your lifespan by up to ten years. Now if that's not a great motivational tool, I don't know what is and as a motivator, we'd all welcome a few extra quality years.

5. **Performance targets.** Not everyone has a competitive streak running through them but if you're a 'Type A', achieving sort of person, setting a physical target is guaranteed to light your motivational fire. Your goal could be beating a specific time (or perhaps a rival!) in a race, improving your body composition percentage ratio so that you carry more muscle than body-fat, or lifting a challenging weight in the gym. Even if the idea of competition doesn't overly excite you, having a meaningful target can still help the most unmotivated person improve.

6. **Have fun!** Yes, having fun and enjoying exercising can be a sufficiently good motivator all on its own. Many people just don't enjoy their exercise routines, often because it's become just that; a routine. Exercise and fun can go hand-in-hand and when you achieve that match, you need no further motivation to regularly work out.

SuperTip

When did you last step outside of your comfort zone? If you train for a sport, why not get involved in a complementary activity that long-term, will aid your performance? For gym regulars, if you always hit the CV machines, surprise your body with a weights workout. For runners, why not try Triathlon, which would tap into your good CV system but would also introduce some new challenges. Motivate and rejuvenate!

Be inspired!

During the lead-up week of the Flora London Marathon, I present a range of running seminars at the official exhibition in London and meet countless runners – all with their own personal story to tell regarding what motivated them to take on the challenge of completing 26.2 miles. To a man (and woman), they all have inspirational stories to tell about raising money for charity, overcoming adversity or simply ploughing through the difficulties of progressing their fitness to a level that enabled them to compete. On race day itself, I see runner after runner pushing themselves beyond their normal limits to achieve their personal goal – which is truly inspirational! Although there are many role models in elite sport that can serve as an inspiration for your training, equally, the achievements of non-elite competitors can be equally motivating and I certainly feel inspired when I witness the tremendous efforts of thousands of 'ordinary' runners. There are inspirational people everywhere and millions of strategies to help you get started, keep going or move up with your training because if you haven't got your health and fitness, what have you got?

Inspirational and motivational heroes.

1. **Fat Man Walking.** In 2006, Steve Vaught, an obese American, decided to embark on a journey across the USA on foot, from coast to coast, in a bid to lose weight, regain his confidence and in his own words – get his life back. Steve chronicled his journey on the internet under the name *'Fat Man Walking'* and proved an inspiration to people worldwide with his online diary through which he chronicled his efforts. En route he managed to lose over 100 pounds in bodyweight and gained self esteem and direction. Walking burns in the region of 100 calories per mile so is a great way to kick-start a weight loss programme and although clearly a million miles away from being anything like an elite athlete, Steve's story is truly inspirational.

2. **Paula's world record.** A completely different type of inspirational story is that of our own Paula Radcliffe, who in 2003 put the world record for the marathon on a completely new level with her 2 hours 15 minutes clocking in London. Paula's dedication to training is legendary and the sight of her striding out alone on what all the commentators described as a totally suicidal pace was amazing as she left everyone else in her wake. Such was the magnitude of her performance that day that she achieved the fastest time for the marathon that year by a British person – male or female! Now whilst we can't expect to get anywhere near the extraordinary feats that Paula has produced, her running has motivated thousands of runners worldwide.

3. **Jane's cancer battle.** In 2000, Jane Tomlinson was diagnosed with incurable breast cancer. She then ran numerous half marathon events, the London Marathon, completed an Ironman race (swim 2.4 miles, cycle 112 miles and run a full 26.2 mile marathon – consecutively) and cycled 4,200 miles across America, raising almost £2 million pounds for charity in the process. We all complain about our lot from time to time but the television documentary that followed Jane on her epic trans-America cycle ride illustrated her depth of fortitude and courage as she fought against constant pain from her debilitating and progressive illness with her determination to complete the challenge and raise much needed funds for cancer research. How inspirational is that?

4. **Age is no barrier.** In 2004, Fauja Singh became the oldest competitor to complete the London Marathon – at age 93! He holds the current world record for the over nineties for the distance, at 5 hours and 40 minutes and following his success, he was signed up by a leading sportswear company to front their 'Impossible is Nothing' advertising campaign. Fauja only took up running at the age of 82 and has since completed seven marathons, raising money for various charities in each event. When most people would be welcoming the pipe and slippers, Fauja has shown that age is no barrier to any achievement, truly endorsing the tag line of his sponsors – Impossible is Nothing.

5. **Fat man swimming.** In 2007, Martin Strel, who describes himself as a short, old, fat man; achieved a world record for swimming the entire length of the Amazon, covering 3,274 miles in a mere 66 days! That equates to swimming the English Channel nearly 3 times a day for almost 10 weeks! En route he battled against extremes of temperature, poisonous fish and crocodiles – aside from the physical challenge of swimming such a huge distance and lost over 32 pounds in bodyweight en route. Strel's physique is actually well suited to the demands of his chosen activity for both buoyancy and warmth and he has demonstrated that although few of us can aspire to being physically ideal, we can still achieve amazing things through sheer determination and hard work.

So what's your personal inspiration? Whilst some of the challenges above are quite extreme, they all demonstrate that age, size, fitness and illness need not be a barrier to achieving your personal goals at your own personal level. Be inspired!

Just do it!

Just do it! is a very famous strap line from an extremely well-known sportswear manufacturer and it perfectly encapsulates that motivational 'can-do' attitude that's synonymous with getting out there and taking part. However, therein lies the problem. Many people find it extremely difficult to take that all important step, whether it's starting out on the road to fitness, returning after a lay-off or even if you do some exercise, keeping the continuity going by avoiding opportunities to procrastinate about available time, the weather, other commitments, etc, etc. We're all past masters at finding 'other things to occupy our time' when deep in our heart of hearts we know what we should be doing.

So, here are some motivations that are sure to strike a chord with you, compressed into a single motivating sentence:

Motivations to just do it!

To . . . ***Increase my energy levels*** to ***Achieve more*** and ***Make everyday tasks easy*** so that I can ***Keep up with the kids,*** enjoy ***Easy weight management*** alongside ***Guilt-free chocolate eating*** so that ***I feel good*** and ***Improve the quality of my life*** which will ***Help to reverse the aging process*** and ***Reduce my risk of suffering from preventable diseases,*** which all in all ***WILL MAKE ME FEEL ALIVE!***

How good is all that! So, if you've still got a stumbling block, below are a list of the five most common reasons for not working out, coupled with strategies to help you focus on what really matters:

The Top 5 excuses for not exercising

1. **I'm too busy!** This is the number one reason that people use for not exercising but if you really want to do something, you'll find the time – whatever. Whether that means getting up earlier to complete a workout, fitting something in at lunchtime, incorporating exercise into your commute, going out late in the evening because your training is important to you because if you really want to you'll sacrifice something. Television, an extra half hour in bed or whatever, the key is to focus upon your goal, write it down, plan how you're going to achieve it and exactly what you need to do and then make the effort.

2. **I'm too unfit!** If you do feel that you're too unfit then it's never been more important for you to take action! There is a common misconception that gyms are stuffed to the gills with super-fit elite athletes without an ounce of surplus flesh anywhere, all wearing the very latest and trendy gear and completing the most arduous of workouts that would challenge even an Olympic champion. Well,

nothing could be further from the truth because modern gyms are full of everyday people working towards their own personal fitness goals. If you're still unsure, link up with an exercise professional to support and guide you towards your targets.

3. **It's too hot/cold/windy/wet, etc.** Come on! We live in the UK and it's frequently wet, occasionally hot or cold and yes the weather can be a right nuisance. But that's as far as it goes. For indoor training, well you've only got the travel to negotiate which is easy and if your chosen activity is outdoors, we live in such a high-tech era that there is a veritable plethora of specialist breathable, or wicking garments that can make a massive difference to your exercise session, either keeping you warm and dry or helping you stay cool and comfortable. So, a trip down to your local sports retailer will ensure that weather conditions excuses become a thing of the past!

4. **I don't know what to do.** Now this one is quite understandable because if you're unused to exercise, have not worked out for some time, are older or perhaps have a medical condition then rushing straight out for a workout is just what you shouldn't be doing. Your training should be correctly tailored to you, your current fitness levels, any pre-conditions and of course your personal goals. Hence, you should ensure that you are comprehensively assessed prior to exercising and that you are instructed in perfect technique, married with correct training protocols so that your workouts are safe, you don't risk injury and you build your fitness at an appropriate pace for you – and not anyone else.

5. **I'll start next week/month/year.** Aaahh yes, the Granddaddy of excuses. It's so easy to put off your plans until tomorrow or later with the limpest of excuses but taking that first step and then simply repeating it with regular continuity will change you from a conscientious objector to an evangelical convert! It's that easy!

Nutrition

'You wouldn't run your car engine on paraffin . . .' **MIKE SEARLE**

The trouble with healthy eating . . .

Everyone loves to enjoy a good meal and these days, as consumers, we are overwhelmed with food choices, not all of which contribute to a healthy nutrition plan. Step into any Supermarket and you will find literally thousands of food products stacked high on the shelves and increasingly, more and more ready meals and processed food options. One of the problems is that 21st century lifestyles are often less conducive to following a healthy eating plan compared with previous generations, with 10 barriers that people find typically prevent them from following eating healthily.

Let's, look at and challenge some of those 10 barriers and suggest healthy eating solutions.

Healthy eating barriers – and solutions

1. **I've got no will power.** This is the most popular barrier to healthy eating and not an easy one to crack. If you're struggling to remain on the straight and narrow, try making small, gradual changes rather than bold sweeping ones because the smaller changes will be easier to integrate into your life. Also, rather than 'go it alone', involve friends and family members in your healthy eating changes so that you've got some support.

2. **Healthy products are too expensive.** Yes, it's true, some healthier foods can cost more but take a look at the price of convenience foods and they are very costly because you're paying for the convenience rather than what's actually in the product.

3. **I'm too busy to eat healthily.** Well, everyone's busy these days and if you're out and about and always on the go, try strategies such as taking healthy snacks like fruit with you and making a packed lunch to take out so that you're not tempted by less healthy choices when you're low on energy.

4. **Cooking takes too long.** Cooking a meal from scratch does take longer than activating the microwave but you can still prepare a home-cooked meal quickly. Pasta is both quick and easy and not every meal has to be cordon bleu!

5. **Buying individual ingredients is more expensive.** For a 'one-off' meal, buying a long list of ingredients can be expensive but with a little ingenuity, those ingredients can be used for other meals as well – spreading the cost very thinly.

6. **It's impossible to eat '5-a-day'.** If you find it hard to hit the target of eating five portions of fruit and vegetables each day then try the following menu ideas, which all count towards your total:

    a. Fruit juice at breakfast.
    b. Fresh fruit added to your breakfast cereal.
    c. A mid-morning fruit snack.
    d. A jacket potato at lunchtime.
    e. Carrot sticks to snack on in the afternoon.
    f. An evening meal with two or three vegetable portions.
    g. In addition, just topping up with fruit throughout the day is simple and convenient and will keep your totals up.

7. **My working hours make eating healthily difficult.** Okay - but you have to eat at some time, so why go for fast food or less healthy options? Planning ahead is the solution here by ensuring that you've got non-processed food choices to hand which will help you avoid temptation and also to make the effort when you aren't working so that you strike a good balance.

8. **Fresh food goes out of date too quickly.** That's true and the longer fresh produce is on the shelf, the more vitamins and minerals leech out of it, so when you do buy fresh food, it's important to use it as soon as possible in order to get maximum nutritional benefits from it. However, if that's just not practical for you then opt for more frozen vegetables because they're frozen immediately after picking and so lose very few of their nutrients before you use them.

9. **My work leaves me too busy to cook.** Sadly, this is a typical problem for so many people who with increasing work commitments, can be either too busy or too tired to prepare a meal when they get home from work. Realistically, that's likely to happen to lots of people from time to time, so if whipping up a pan of quick-cook pasta doesn't appeal, then simply take some time out for proper cooking when you have more time such as weekends and perhaps on Friday evenings.

10. **I'm not sure what I should be buying.** This is a real problem because there is a plethora of conflicting evidence and hearsay regarding what does and doesn't constitute healthy eating. Food

manufacturers can add to the problem with confusing labelling and it can be difficult to sort the wheat from the chaff. The easiest solution is to try and stick to the following guideline: avoid pre-packaged, processed food choices and you're well on the way to a healthy nutrition plan.

Eat yourself fit!

The most common target that I hear is to lose weight. Although diet may not commonly be perceived to be part of your Fitness Programme, it is actually fundamental in order to correctly fuel the body for daily activities, growth and repair. For example, how would a marathon runner fare if they hadn't loaded up at the pre-race pasta party the night before and would a bodybuilder succeed in bulking up their muscles if their protein intake was insufficient? These two examples may be slightly extreme for many people but illustrate the importance of a carefully balanced Nutrition Programme to run alongside your Fitness Programme.

However weight loss alone is an unbalanced picture. Through appropriate toning exercise, you can actually gain weight, yet still improve your shape. I have personally witnessed a lady who had a goal of losing weight actually gaining 6 pounds and dropping a whole dress size at the same time! This shows how focusing on weight loss alone or indeed just exercise alone does not give you the best chance of achieving your goals. Combining the two is the optimum strategy to achieve your health and fitness goals and importantly, to maintain a long-term healthy lifestyle.

So, what factors should you be considering when thinking about a healthy diet? Nutrition is an enormous subject but to start with a few pointers, here are the top four Golden Nutrition Rules.

1. **Always eat breakfast.** After fasting all night, kick-start your body's engine with some good quality food. If you ever feel lethargic in the morning, or skip breakfast and are ravenous by 10 o'clock, you will feel 100% better with some food when you get up. Top of the breakfast charts is porridge, perhaps topped with fresh or dried fruit. Porridge will provide you with sustained energy and cancel out the 10 o'clock 'munchies'! Cereals provide a simple and quick breakfast fix but try and avoid sugar or chocolate coated varieties.

2. **Hydrate.** Symptoms of dehydration include unusual fatigue, dizziness, hunger, dry skin, dark urine and general lethargy. When you consider that the majority of our bodies are made up from water, topping up your body's fluid intake with water and natural fluids (eg: fruit juice) is extremely important.

3. **Take the *'20 per day'* test.** Try and eat 20 different (and healthy!) foods each day to ensure that you are fuelling your body with a broad range of different nutrients to ensure that you are getting the full complement of vitamins, minerals and trace elements – and your meals are interesting too!

4. **Avoid eating late at night.** Breakfast like a King, lunch like a Prince and dine like a Pauper is an old adage but there is some truth in the saying. Many people commonly 'end-of-day load' their food intake, sometimes eating a large evening meal at 9 o'clock at night, having eaten very sparingly throughout the day. Effectively they have starved themselves during their period of maximum activity and when they get home they are extremely hungry and eat a very large meal before going to bed.

A correctly structured nutrition plan in combination with a correctly prescribed fitness programme is the only sure-fire way to long-term health and fitness and following the 4 Golden Rules is a good way to start helping your health!

SuperTip

If it comes in a packet, leave it on the Supermarket shelf. Processed foods usually have many of the nutrients removed and many undesirable ingredients such as 'E' numbers added in the factory. Try and limit your intake of processed food and substitute fresh or whole-food choices wherever possible.

The best to you each morning?

A diet high in salt is a proven contributory factor to high blood pressure and cardiovascular disease, two of the most common causes of illness and death in the UK. Also, high levels of salt in your diet has been found to have many other negative effects on health, including osteoporosis, stomach cancer and asthma. Campaigners have been lobbying breakfast cereal manufacturers to limit salt in their foods for a long time, because many cereals still contain more salt than a bag of crisps! The Food Standards Agency has set a target for adults to consume a maximum of 6 grams of salt per day, which could save 35,000 lives each year from heart attacks and strokes, equating to saving the life of one person every 15 minutes, every hour, every day – an awesome statistic. Around 80% of the salt that we consume is 'hidden', ie: it is added to foods during processing, with the remaining 20% added during cooking or at the table. To reduce your salt intake, focus upon the following tips and help your health.

Top tips for reducing salt in your diet

1. **Wean yourself off salt gradually.** If your palate has become accustomed to a high salt intake, at first meals may taste a little bland. Reduce your salt intake gradually and within 3 weeks your taste receptors will become much more sensitive to flavours and you'll soon find food tasting much better.

2. **Choose lower salt products at the supermarket.** A huge number of ready-made foods contain salt, including a few surprising entries such as cakes, flour, most tinned products, sauces, soups and bread. Have a look at a few food labels and you will notice how many common foods contain salt, often at very high levels. Try and limit your selection of highly salted products.

3. **Compare foods when shopping.** Nowadays, we are overwhelmed with choice and information, giving us the opportunity to compare products when shopping. As a guide, 0.5 grams of salt per 100 grams of a food is high for salt content, whilst 0.1 grams per 100 grams of food is much better for health. So, simply seek out those low salt alternatives to improve your diet.

4. **Limit foods naturally high in salt.** There are some non-processed foods that are naturally high in salt, so to reduce your intake, limit consumption of Seafood, Kidneys, Celery and Chicory.

5. **Don't add salt to cooking.** If you add salt to meals during cooking, try leaving it out and enhancing the dishes by using herbs and spices. This will give you a greater range of flavours rather than simply a salty flavour that you are used to.

6. **Leave the salt pot in the cupboard.** If you always have the salt pot on the table, it becomes a habit to add salt to food – whether you need it or not. If the salt pot is in the cupboard, you have to actively decide that your meal needs salt before you add it.

So, check-out your diet and ensure that you 'get the best each morning and for all your meals.

Performance & Competition

> *'You can't train like I do AND go out with girls'.*
> ***JOAQUIM CRUZ, OLYMPIC GOLD MEDALLIST***

Use your brain to train!

You might think that mental preparation isn't relevant to you if you're not involved in competitive activities but having the right mindset for a training session is extremely important too. For example, when faced with a physical challenge, such as lifting a heavier weight in the gym, or continuing to maintain a pace when starting to feel tired, typically, people are either 'Associators' or 'Disassociators'. This means that when experiencing discomfort, they either focus on what they are trying to achieve (Associators) or think about something else (Disassociators) – to take their minds off the discomfort! Studies have shown that the Associators achieve higher levels of performance, demonstrating that adopting the correct mental approach is very valuable. Obviously our brains control our bodies and within limits, our bodies will carry out the instructions that our brains send out.

So how can you adopt a positive mental attitude to help prepare yourself for training? To begin with, try and avoid a haphazard 'spur-of-the-moment' approach and at some point in the day before your activity, think about what you are going to be doing and when and how you are going to do it. That alone will be beneficial by ensuring that you arrive at your Gym or Club with a clear idea of your goal. Finally, follow the tip below, which will help maximise the benefits that you gain from whatever exercise you enjoy.

SuperTip

Before you rush out for your next bout of training, try spending a few moments beforehand focusing on what you want and intend to achieve from your session. Clear your mind of other tasks and problems and totally direct your efforts towards your goal. By totally focusing on the activity, you will find that your levels of stress are reduced, your performance is improved and your overall enjoyment is enhanced!

Be your BEST!

Preparing correctly in the run-up to an important event can mean the difference between success and failure: either hitting a personal target or struggling into the finish the worse for wear. This preparation is relevant to any sport, any activity and even each training session, so if you want to 'be your best', follow the tips below to maximise the benefits that you get from your exercise sessions.

8 simple strategies to help you 'Be your BEST'

1. **Rest.** Frequently the most neglected element of a training programme, sufficient rest allows your body to recover and repair from an earlier session and also ensures that your mind is fresh for the demands of your next training session or event.

2. **Mental rehearsal.** Going through a routine of what your session or race requires will effectively programme what you are targeting to achieve. Forewarned is forearmed and you don't want any surprises on the day.

3. **Keep positive.** It is very important to keep positive – whatever happens. Problems such as unfavourable weather conditions, a cancelled exercise class or your favourite piece of gym equipment being monopolised by someone else can all be resolved. Focus on what you can do, not what you can't.

4. **Attention to detail.** The devil's in the detail is a well known saying and focusing on all the little things that will make your race or session run smoothly will have a big impact upon your final performance. For example, is your kit tried, tested and guaranteed not to chafe over 26.2 miles, or have you packed your favourite post gym workout sports drink in your kitbag?

5. **Know what you want to achieve.** Before you begin your workout, do you know exactly what you're going to do and what you want to get out of your specific exercise session. If you drift into your session aimlessly and unfocused, you will not get the most out of the time you have committed to your workout. It is valuable to spend a few moments thinking about and planning what you are going to do so that your time is spent profitably.

6. **Enlist help and support.** If you feel pressurised to cut your session short perhaps because of family commitments, your focus will be dissipated; whereas if your family and friends understand the importance of your race / training, then they can offer you support, allowing you to focus on quality, rather than the clock.

7. **Be prepared to work hard.** Go into your session or event with the attitude that you will put in the effort necessary to be your best. To achieve that, you will need to work hard, so instruct your mind that you intend to work to the best of your ability, with the carrot that you will enjoy the results afterwards.

8. **Do your thing.** The gym, exercise class or race is full of people lifting a heavier weight, working at a different tempo or running at a different intensity. None of that matters to you because you are solely there for yourself and to complete your session or race, not anyone else's. Avoid getting sucked into an unsuitable pace, doing an unfamiliar exercise or straining to match someone else's performance. Do your thing and be your best.

SuperTip

In the 1968 Olympics, 400 metre hurdler David Hemery won the gold medal in a new world record time – the ultimate performance for any athlete. Afterwards, when interviewed, he said that for weeks before the race, he had visualised every possible combination of lane draw, opponent, conditions and his position in the field. When he actually came to run the race, whatever scenario he was faced with, he already had it taped – in his mind – and knew exactly how to react. Hence he produced a fantastic performance. By spending time before your event going through a range of different scenarios, you too will 'have it taped', and at whatever level you perform, you'll be able to 'Be your BEST' as well.

Posture

> *'I am often confronted with patients who suffer chronic pain as a result of the consequences of poor posture'.*
>
> ***NHS GP***

Stand up for fitness!

These days, bad posture and posture related problems are endemic; predominantly due to changes in lifestyle. For example, it is common to spend the majority of the day seated, either at the wheel of a car, in front of the television or chained to a computer; each of which contributes to bad posture. If you have poor posture, your muscles struggle to hold you up and fatigue develops, which causes muscle imbalances as you try to ease the load on your body. You then waste energy just moving and you feel stiff and immobile, which traps you in a cycle of similar problems.

For example; back problems are usually the result of long-term muscular postural problems, which can lead to degenerative osteoarthritis in later years and with approximately 13 million working days lost annually solely due to back pain, it's a serious issue.

However, there is a great deal that you can do address postural problems by making small modifications to your lifestyle:

Lifestyle tips for good posture

1. **Watch your weight.** Excess weight is a major contributor to postural problems, particularly when it's sited around the stomach region. It will result in weakened abdominal muscles, combined with tightness and discomfort in the lower back; so by ensuring that you aren't carrying any excess load, you're reducing your chances of lower back pain.

2. **Work out – carefully!** A correctly prescribed programme of regular exercise is key to lifelong good posture but it is just as important that your programme is balanced and includes both resistance training and stretching exercises, so that you are strong and flexible.

3. **And so to bed!** You literally spend years of your life in bed, so if your mattress is unsupportive, you're contributing to bad posture whilst you're asleep. The solution is to buy a firm mattress which

supports your spine and helps maintain the shape that a person with good upright posture achieves.

4. **Mind how you go.** Accidents, falls and injuries can have a long-term affect on how you move and cause imbalances within the body. Get any injuries checked out and don't forget those ones that you had years ago which may still be contributing to postural imbalances.

5. **Watch your back!** In addition to focusing on your exercise and movements, it is very important to consider your back. Any lifting should be done with a straight back; using the legs to take the load. Also, avoid 'touching the toes' exercises, which is totally contraindicated and can easily lead to slipped disc or other long-term back problems. If your back is strong, then you have one of the pieces of the good postural jigsaw in place.

6. **Train your core.** Core exercises build strength in your body's chassis, the framework on which everything else is supported and also help train you in achieving good posture during your everyday movements because you become so much more aware of your body and its position.

7. **Sleep well.** The optimum sleeping position is on your back, with a pillow under your head, not your shoulders; so that your neck is correctly aligned. You may also find it more comfortable to place a pillow underneath your knees, which can limit any lower back discomfort.

8. **Be seated.** Many people spend long hours working at a desk, so good ergonomics is very important. Try and sit upright, with both feet flat on the floor, adjusting your chair height so that there is no undue strain anywhere around the body. Also, don't just sit there; get up for frequent breaks to loosen up, which will also help you keep alert and maintain concentration.

Pregnancy

> *'Pregnancy is a natural condition, not an illness'.*
>
> **BETTER HEALTH AGENCY**

Paula's pregnant pause . . .

One of the big news stories in the running world over recent years was that of marathon world record holder Paula Radcliffe's pregnancy. Arguably the most dedicated athlete in the UK, Paula's happy event raised some interesting questions; including how would she cope with having to back off from her formidable training regime and could she return to competing at the highest level after her baby was born?

Paula's dedication and commitment to training is well documented and typically includes three training sessions per day, which during peak periods can total up to 140 miles per week. This is in addition to specific resistance training, flexibility work, core exercises, lengthy periods on the massage couch, mental rehearsal and her famed two sleeps per day for up to 12 hours. Putting this volume of training to one side was obviously tough but history indicates that on returning to running, elite female athletes can actually perform at an even higher level, borne out by former elite female runners Ingrid Kristiansen and Sonia O'Sullivan, who enjoyed tremendous success following childbirth. Not everyone who is pregnant plans to run marathons relatively soon after giving birth but keeping fit is still important because it helps weight management and studies at the University of Iowa have found that women who exercise regularly throughout pregnancy had easier and shorter labours.

However, there are precautions which you need to consider when you are pregnant for a safe and fit, nine months!

Top exercising tips when pregnant

1. **Keep well hydrated.** As your body changes, you may find that you sweat more so carry a water bottle in the gym and when doing CV workouts to keep your fluid levels topped up.

2. **Wear it well!** Choose comfortable, loose-fitting clothing because loose clothing will help keep you cool, particularly as your shape changes.

3. **Allow longer recoveries.** Some days you'll be overflowing with energy and on other days, everything can seem a huge effort. With

your energy levels fluctuating, remember to take extra rest whenever you feel you need to.

4. **Be thorough.** Always complete a thorough warm-up and cool-down in your session. Pregnancy affects your circulatory system, so extend both your warm-up and cool-down to 15 minutes so that your body gradually adapts to your exercise session.

5. **Watch your back (1).** As your baby grows, your back comes under an increasing load, so always consider your body position, particularly if carrying out resistance training exercises.

6. **Watch your back (2).** After 20 weeks, if exercising in a supine position (lying on your back), you can experience dizziness, numbness at the extremities and a lack of oxygen to the foetus, so avoid any exercises of this type.

7. **Avoid over-stretching.** Your joints gradually become looser as your pregnancy develops, so avoid excessive flexibility exercises that could over-stretch muscles and tendons.

8. **Consider your energy requirements.** Combining exercise with pregnancy increases your calorie requirements so pay particular attention to your pre and post exercise nutritional needs. Eating for two' is now considered unnecessary but it is important that you correctly fuel both your baby's growth and your workout.

9. **Choose low impact aerobic activities.** To avoid excessive pounding and also damage to slacker joints, try activities such as swimming and cycling and only jog if you jogged prior to your pregnancy.

10. **Choose appropriate footwear.** Good ankle and foot support is important, particularly in later pregnancy as joints become more lax, so make sure that your trainers are both cushioned and have sufficient support.

11. **Avoid contact sports.** Activities that could result in collisions and/or potential damage to the mother and baby should always be avoided.

12. **Focus on correct posture and technique at all times.** It is important to put extra focus into your movements and posture because as your shape changes, your body is loaded in different ways. If you enjoy working out with weights, correct technique is vital to ensure a safe exercise session.

Easy does is it . . .

Following the birth of your baby, your return to activity, exercise and your usual weight should be carefully structured to facilitate the changes that your body has encountered and the likely higher levels of fatigue that you will probably be experiencing (all parents will know exactly what this means!).

So, for a safe return to exercise and activity post pregnancy, follow these top eight post-natal tips:

Top 8 post-natal exercise tips

1. **The first 6 weeks.** Whether you're a first time mother or you've got a new addition to your family, the early weeks are always a period of adjustment, so resist any temptation to throw yourself headlong into any form of exercise. You should allow yourself a minimum of six weeks before you consider returning to exercise or improving your fitness. If your baby has been delivered by caesarean section then you should give yourself more time, allowing a minimum of eight weeks before you consider exercising.

2. **Speak to your Health Visitor.** Your Health Visitor is a useful 'first port of call' to discuss your return to exercise and will be able to offer you specific advice relevant to you, the length of your labour, type of delivery, etc.

3. **Stretch – carefully.** Flexibility should always be a component of everyone's fitness programme but after giving birth you need to be cautious in your approach to stretching. A key factor to consider is the hormone relaxin; which is responsible for softening ligaments and cartilage so that your tissues can expand and stretch to accommodate the growing baby. Relaxin remains in the body for many months after delivery and if the joints are excessively extended after pregnancy then permanent damage could occur. Hence it is important that before you begin exercising that your functional flexibility is comprehensively assessed so as to avoid injury.

4. **Watch those weights!** Following on from the effects of relaxin in your body, it is also vital that your resistance training is carried out with care and perfect technique. Resistance training will be extremely beneficial because it is essential to re-tone up muscles and rebuild your strength but incorrect technique and an inappropriate weight, combined with any joint instability could similarly result in injury, so care and advice is necessary.

5. **Low impact!** Impact activities such as jogging and running are excellent for rebuilding your cardiovascular fitness and maintaining your bone density in your lower skeleton but so as to avoid the risk of bone and joint injuries, limit these activities to walking for the first few months. In addition to walking; good alternative cardiovascular activities include cycling, swimming, gym machines such as the cross-trainer, stationary bike and rower and these will also serve as a valuable prelude to more challenging exercise later.

6. **Activate those abs!** During your pregnancy, your abdominal muscles will have become stretched and weakened, so this is a key area to target. Not only will it help you regain your shape but it will also reduce the load on your lower back (it is extremely common for women to suffer from lower back pain in the final trimester because of the increased load at the front of the body, which cause the lower back muscles to be in a constantly contracted state).

7. **More core!** Carrying out core training exercises will not only help you to regain your shape – and fast but will also significantly improve your posture and overall body awareness, so they are a key element of your routine. Try to incorporate a combination of static and rotational type exercises (using a stability ball), so that you build strength and control.

8. **Don't forget your pelvic floor.** Your body can take quite a battering during childbirth so it is essential that you practise your pelvic floor exercises repeatedly, post delivery. Regular pelvic floor muscle training will give you the complete bladder control that you enjoyed pre pregnancy and of course the beauty of these exercises is that they can be carried out absolutely anywhere – in fact no-one will realise that you're actually doing them!

Returning to Fitness

> *'Allow double the time of your absence to return to previous fitness levels'.*
> **MIKE SEARLE**

Back to school = back to fitness

When the school summer holidays are over, for many people it will be back to the usual routine of ferrying the children everywhere and all the organising that comes with it! The long summer holidays are a great time for some family relaxation, a break from the routines of school and work and the opportunity to recharge your batteries. However, getting back in the school run routine does have some benefits. Term-time brings a lot of structure to the week and provides the opportunity to get back into that exercise habit and of course - enjoy all the benefits that regular exercise brings. These include weight management, more energy, better sleep, better appetite and feeling good all over!

So, if you're thinking about getting back into your fitness routine after the summer, then simply follow the Back to Fitness Tips below, to help you ease back into your training safely and effectively.

Back to Fitness tips

1. **Go Light.** If you usually weight-train, then for your first couple of sessions, reduce the weight that you lift, or reduce the number of repetitions – or both. This will help you avoid post-workout muscle stiffness and soreness. Gradually increase the weight and repetitions towards your previous levels and soon your body will adapt to training and you will be able to return to your usual workout.

2. **Run slowly.** For runners, take your first week back training much easier, just doing steady, comfortable runs. Once you've got a week or two of foundation miles under your belt, then step up the intensity of you feel like it. If you dive straight back into high intensity training, not only is it extremely hard but your risk of injury is increased because you have lost some of your previous condition.

3. **Don't forget flexibility.** Exercise downtime and reduced levels of activity will result in a reduction in your previous mobility and flexibility. If your body has not been challenged so much and your general activity has not needed much mobility and flexibility, then

you can feel sluggish and immobile. To counteract any feelings of stiffness, make time for some extra flexibility work. It will make your whole body feel looser and lighter as well as improving your performance and reducing your risk of injury.

4. **Think of the benefits!** It may be that you're struggling to motivate yourself to return to exercise, if you've lost that consistency of your regular sessions. Unfortunately the gains that you make from your training quickly disappear if you don't exercise regularly, so the sooner you make that commitment again, the better! Just think back to how much better you felt when you exercised, whether it's looking good, keeping your weight down or feeling energised and kick-start your routine now!

5. **Treat your muscles!** If you find that you do slightly overdo it on your return to training, perhaps experiencing some post-exercise soreness or the odd twinge, try treating yourself to a sports massage. A good sports massage will flush out all the waste by-products of exercise and really invigorate your muscles, which in turn will invigorate your workouts. Gone will be any stiffness and soreness and additionally, your muscles and entire body will function more efficiently. Your first training session after a massage will feel great – and your performance will be improved.

Returning to training sensibly = A return to previous fitness levels sooner + Injury avoidance. Additionally, you will enjoy the challenge of getting fitter – which in itself is a great motivator as you see improvements.

Back to school will no longer be a headache, it'll mean Back to Fitness!

SuperTip

Exercise should be fun and enjoyable and if you've had a lay-off, the last thing you want after your first session is sore muscles. A lay-off often re-motivates you but avoid overdoing it because you are keen to get fit again. It won't take long for you to make up the lost ground. When you return to training, re-introduce your body gradually to activity so that you don't spend the next couple of days walking around like a robot because you're so stiff!

Resistance Training

> *'My strength is as the strength of ten because my heart is pure'.*
> ***A. Tennyson***

Play the weighting game

It is now recommended that adults complete two (yes two!!) resistance training sessions per week. Immediately, I can hear the collective whys and what fors? Well, working out with weights is of paramount importance for everyone, irrespective of age, sex and any other health and fitness goals, in order to maintain strength, muscle mass, posture, burn calories and execute daily tasks without difficulty. As we age (and by aging I mean after approximately 30 years old), nature dictates that we will lose muscle mass, with a consequent loss of strength and postural control - unless we take appropriate remedial action; ie: regular resistance training workouts.

So, if you're looking to correctly structure your training or if you've never been to a gym before then follow these ten steps to successful weight-training:

Ten steps to successful weight-training

1. **Assessment time!** Before you start, it is vital that your overall health, current state of fitness, posture, muscle imbalances and any medical conditions or contraindications are comprehensively assessed. This will ensure that it is both safe for you to commence training and also that your training can be correctly structured for you.

2. **Get professional.** Which specific exercises are best for you? How should you structure your training for maximum gains, also taking into account your personal fitness levels, goals, etc? How should you train? How often should you train? How much rest should you take between exercises? There are a multitude of questions and potential pitfalls when you begin but by getting professional help, not only will you train in safety but you'll also get the most out of your training time and you'll participate rather than just attending your training sessions.

3. **Do the right thing!** With resistance training, technique is king. Ignore correct technique and at best you won't progress because you aren't carrying out exercises correctly. At worst you'll end up

injured, which will put paid to all your health and fitness plans. For example: I frequently see people in gyms lifting weights without protecting that key area – the back and I always intervene to offer them correct lifting technique advice. So, make sure that you have professional advice and guidance so that you learn correct technique from the outset because it will pay dividends again and again.

4. **Balance out your training.** A very common mistake is to focus upon training the muscle groups that you're best at or you simply prefer. This is frequently compounded by ignoring to train muscles which require more complex exercises – or perhaps you're simply unfamiliar with exercises for certain muscle groups. The problem and danger here is that you will develop imbalances which can affect your posture and lead to injury. So for example, if you exercise your biceps, balance that out with triceps exercises, if you do some chest training, don't forget your upper back, etc.

5. **First gear first.** With that first flush of enthusiasm to get fit, it can be tempting to hit your training with maximum force. However that is likely to end with plenty of sore muscles – or possibly injury if you seriously overdo it. So, start slowly and run through your gearbox slowly, allowing time for your body to steadily adapt to new exercises and new training loads and then you'll get so much more out of your training; long-term.

6. **Rest = progress.** Insufficient rest equates to limited progress or even no progress at all. Rest is the most important component of your training programme and if you neglect it, you won't maximise your training efforts. So, always include at least one complete rest day each week, back off if you feel tired and that way, you'll make consistent gains. Remember, your body only gets the opportunity to rebuild stronger AFTER your training session and if you over-train, your muscles cannot recover and rebuild properly and hence your progress will be halted.

7. **Be patient.** There's no such thing as overnight success, real progress comes from consistent, balanced training, not a training blitz. Gradually increase the frequency & intensity of your workouts and you'll reap the rewards – again – long-term. It is far better to complete one or two workouts each week rather than training every other day for a fortnight and then forgetting about exercising for a month.

8. **Variety is the spice of life.** A common mistake with your training is to do the same thing, the same way, every time you exercise.

Now initially, that'll bring results but your gains will rapidly tail off as your body becomes accustomed to the training stimulus. Thereafter you'll find either limited or zero progress, leading to frustration and a huge drop in motivation. However, spice up your sessions by changing the training stimulus in the form of different exercises, different routines and different methods and your body will rise to each new challenge and you'll find that you continue to make gains year in, year out.

9. **Five minutes stretching.** Now this has nothing to do with the mechanics of resistance training but is still an integral part of your session. After your workout and cool-down, always spend a minimum of five minutes stretching out your muscles. The muscles to focus upon are the ones that you've exercised harder. So for example, if you moved up with your bench press, make sure that you stretch your chest out and similarly, include the muscle groups that have been loaded the most.

10. **Take an exercise holiday.** Yes, this one's for real! Factoring in rest into your training week is key but it does no harm to occasionally miss an entire weeks training. Often, that can coincide with a holiday and is necessary to simply let your body (and mind) recover and get refreshed. Thereafter, when you come back to your workouts, although you may find that your performance has deteriorated slightly, you'll be absolutely raring to go with a renewed incentive to attack your training again.

Women SHOULD work out with weights!

There's a conversation that I frequently have with women and it centres on lifting weights. Women are concerned that if they incorporate resistance training into their sessions they'll *'bulk up/get big muscles/turn into a bodybuilder'* - or similar. Well nothing could be further from the truth! It's a common misconception that if women lift weights then they'll turn into muscle-bound bodybuilders. Without illegal medical intervention combined with untold hours spent each day in the gym, women will never end up with massive muscles – ever! Women are not genetically predisposed to carry a large muscle mass but as with men, they can get tremendous health and fitness benefits from resistance training. In fact, with modern sedentary and labour-saving 21st century lives, working out with weights has never been more important. Resistance training provides a comprehensive range of health and fitness benefits that men but women in particular, can gain from working out with weights.

Top 8 benefits from working out with weights

1. **Greater strength.** It might seem an obvious one but when you consider how labour-saving our lives typically are these days, many people have few opportunities day-to-day to exercise their muscles. Hence, to counteract the *'21st century effect'*, we need to lift weights to maintain strength for optimum health. How many jobs are now computer based, involving sitting at a desk for the majority of the day? Inactivity is the death knell for our muscles and strength and indeed our health as a whole, so we need to reactivate dormant muscles by lifting weights and reclaim back the quality in our lives.

2. **Improved posture.** Our muscles give our bodies support as well as strength and so maintaining good posture is absolutely key to avoid long-term postural aches, pains and associated musculo-skeletal problems. By following a correctly prescribed programme of resistance training to maintain the body in complete balance, postural problems can be overcome and the body realigned.

3. **Counteracting osteoporosis.** Osteoporosis, or brittle bone disease affects both women and men but women are more likely to suffer from bone fractures, particularly as they get older. However, lifting weights actually strengthens the skeleton because the force of muscles and tendons 'pulling' on bones when you lift a weight results in your bone density actually increasing. Hence resistance training is absolutely key for women, not only for muscular strength benefits but to strengthen the skeleton to reduce the risk of osteoporosis.

4. **Tone up.** Whilst men may be looking more to build muscle mass to achieve a defined and muscular look, women typically want to tone up all over. Well, working out with weights is essential if that is one of your goals because whilst you may be able to achieve a slim figure through a combination of cardiovascular exercise and correct nutrition, unless you focus upon all-over toning then everything will sag in the wrong places! So, hit the gym and kick those problem areas into touch!

5. **Burn calories.** Weight loss is a common fitness goal so if you're looking to lose weight then weights are your friend. When you tone up you improve your strength and the increased muscle that you carry burns more calories – all the time! Hence, as part of a balanced workout, resistance training supports weight loss. Whether you're working out or not, more muscle means more

calories burned – every minute of the day, so resistance training for increased calorie burn is an absolute must.

6. **Life becomes easier.** How many times do you make an excuse to have a break from lifting and carrying your children – because you're tired? Or similarly, perhaps an everyday task such as carrying shopping or gardening leaves you worn out? It's easy to fall into the *'well I'm not so young any more'* trap of making an excuse but the truth is that you can improve your strength whatever your age and if you're stronger then all these simple tasks become much, much easier and you can get more out of your life.

7. **Combat Father Time.** Nature dictates that as we get older, we lose muscle mass. However, it doesn't have to be this way. The old adage *'use it or lose it'* has never been more true because if we take steps to counteract this muscle wastage then we can not only slow down these aging effects but actually reverse them! Recent studies in America have found that a regular programme of weight training actually reverses the age related decline normally associated with older people – and the study group were all aged 70 or older!

8. **Improve performance.** For many people, training at the gym is a means to a different end in that they want to get fitter for their chosen sport. Well you can improve in every sport or activity if you're stronger and the beauty of resistance training is that if you have specific sporting goals then your programme can be precisely tailored to the demands and requirements of your sport to improve your performance and enhance your enjoyment of your activity.

SuperTip

Whilst it's clear that working out with weights brings a whole raft of health and fitness benefits, starting out on a conditioning programme needs care. Ensure that you are correctly assessed before you begin so that your training is right for you, your posture, your current fitness levels, age and any medical conditions that you may suffer from. Also, when working out with weights, technique is king, for safety and results, so always ensure that you are taught correct technique and you will progress faster and avoid the risk of injury.

Rest & Recovery

> *'Always have one complete rest day per week'.*
> **DAME TANNI GREY THOMPSON, 11 TIMES PARALYMPIC GOLD MEDALLIST**

Rest, recuperate and rejuvenate

After any competition and also following training, rest and recovery is key. Anyone who is active in sport and exercise needs to factor in a little r & r into their training schedules so look at the following recovery strategies that you can incorporate into your routine so that you remain fresh, avoid over-training and importantly, reduce your risk of injury as well.

Top 10 recuperation strategies

1. **Total rest days**. Everyone, irrespective of their level of training should factor complete rest days into their exercise schedules so that they can recover both physically and mentally from the demands of training. Rather than lose fitness as many addicted exercisers feel, you will find that you can progress much further and your fitness gains will be more sustainable.

2. **Sports massage.** Exercise stresses the body and when carried out repeatedly, can cause micro tears in the muscles and intra-muscular adhesions to form – which reduce the muscle functionality and can lead to injury. Regular sports massage will flush out the waste by-products of your training, break down adhesions, re-align muscle fibres and ensure that your muscles remain fully functional so that injury is far less likely.

3. **Sleep.** The value of sleep should not be underestimated and is particularly important if you have increased your training load. Nowadays it is common to forgo sleep as we try and cram additional activities into our 24 hours but when you are rested, your performance in every arena is improved, not just the sporting one, so don't neglect your sleep.

4. **Recovery days.** A recovery day is one where you forget about the stopwatch or the structured programme and simply *'go-as-you-please'*. You don't have to stop your training, just back off on the intensity so that you're refreshed for your next challenging session.

5. **Cross-training.** Cross-training is carrying out an alternative exercise activity that supports your primary activity but ensures that you avoid overload. For example a runner might build cycling training into their week or someone who lifts weights might row to improve their CV fitness. As well as giving you all round fitness benefits, cross-training helps you prevent staleness by always doing the same activity week-in, week-out.

6. **Variety.** If you always do the same sort of exercise, the same way, you'll soon find boredom creeping in and your motivation flagging. Hence it is a great idea to constantly change your workout, training routes and exercises because you'll find that not only do you remain mentally fresh, you fitness will progress faster because of the ever changing stimulus that your body has to adapt to.

7. **Post exercise nutrition (1).** To accelerate your recovery, make sure that you consume something like a sports drink within the first 15 minutes of completing your exercise session. This is the period where your body is super receptive to refuelling and so if you take advantage of this window, you'll fast-track your recovery.

8. **Post exercise nutrition (2).** The second fuelling factor to support your recovery is to consume a meal containing both complex carbohydrate and protein within 2 hours of completing your workout which will further support your refuelling and the protein will help the rebuilding process.

9. **A complete break.** Now you might think this is surprising but a total break from exercise is sometimes exactly what's needed to recharge your batteries. Elite athletes will shut down completely after a strenuous event of at the end of a season and simply allow their bodies to fully recover from the stresses and strains of repeated performance. So a holiday could be the ideal time to rejuvenate after a tough season and then when you return to training, you'll be raring to go.

10. **Eat protein.** Now it's important that you consume a balanced diet including complex carbohydrates, protein and fats but I frequently see people who exercise focusing upon carbohydrate and consuming insufficient amounts of protein to support their training. It's not just bodybuilders who need to eat protein – anyone who works out needs to ensure that they are consuming enough to support growth and repair and even if your training is mainly CV based – such as a runner, you still need good quality protein.

Running

> *'Now bid me run and I will strive with things impossible'.*
> ***W. Shakespeare***

Exercise – I'd run a mile!

Even in these days of metric measurements, the mile is still a classic athletics distance, with a history dating back to before Roger Bannister's record breaking efforts in 1954, when he became the first person to run under four minutes for 1760 yards. Although the mile has now been usurped by the 1500 metres, the distance is still the benchmark that middle distance runners measure themselves against, even today. For anyone starting out on the fitness path, being able to run a mile non-stop is an ideal target. Once you can complete a mile without taking a walking break, you are firmly on the road to improved fitness. If you're unused to training, the idea of running a mile might be anathema but it's surprising how rapidly your horizons can change once you see the tangible returns of improved fitness and well-being that regular cardiovascular exercise brings.

Running a mile is genuinely in reach of most people so if you fancy testing your fitness, simply follow the training tips below and get ready for your mile.

Training for the mile.

1. **Get a check-up!** If you haven't exercised for some time, have any medical conditions or are unsure about beginning an exercise programme then before you begin, link up with an exercise professional or visit your GP to get the all clear first.

2. **Get some shoes!** Running is one of the cheapest fitness activities and you probably already own most of the basic kit items that you need to get started. Shorts and a t-shirt are all you need in the way of kit when you are beginning but it is important to purchase some proper running shoes. Good running shoes are not just fancy trainers, they are an investment in your running health because they will protect against injury and repay you again and again with the comfort that they will provide for your training. Modern shoes will last for at least 500 miles so you'll certainly get your money's worth out of them.

3. **Get a stopwatch!** Monitoring and recording your fitness progression is a great motivational tool and it is worth spending a couple of pounds on a basic stopwatch. With consistent training, you'll be amazed over the coming weeks how your distance can increase and your times reduce and sometimes in the same session!

4. **Get going!** Now you're ready to begin. First, measure out a mile route from your home, either in your car or perhaps on a bike with a mileometer. Next, start your stopwatch and set out on your first training session. You can walk, jog or run, whatever you wish. For your initial workout, see how far you can progress along your measured mile. Record your time and how far you have managed.

5. **Put your feet up!** The day after your first training session should be a rest day to allow your body to recover from your first session. Rest is the most important (and frequently the most neglected) component of a training programme because it is only when you rest that your body can rebuild and adapt to the increased load that you have subjected it to. Cumulative training without adequate rest is the sure-fire route to injury and illness.

6. **Keep going!** For your second training session, your minimum target is to match the distance that you achieved on your first outing. Ideally, you will manage a little further. Record your time again. You should continue working towards completing a mile with a combination of walking, jogging or running until you can complete the entire distance non-stop. Target three sessions per week and you will be pleasantly surprised at how rapidly you will move towards completing your first mile.

7. **Upward and onward!** Once you have that first mile under your belt, you should aim to not only complete it non-stop but to complete it jogging or running. Again, carefully and gradually increase the duration that you jog and run, and your target is jogging or running the mile without stopping. By recording all your times with your stopwatch, measuring your progression is easy and also extremely motivating.

8. **The event!** Providing that you adopt a careful and structured approach, a seven week lead-in to testing yourself over a mile will take you to the start line prepared and confident that you can run your mile and have enjoy the day.

Race for YOUR life!

There are hundreds of thousands of women for whom a specific date each June becomes a serious target. During the summer months, these women will don their training shoes and take to the roads and lanes for the annual Race for Life 5K. What started out a few years ago as a very low-key event has now blossomed into a nationwide race series boasting in excess of 160 different venues around the country and over 150,000 participants. Some women race for personal best times, others to raise money for Cancer Research, some run in memory of friends and relatives who have succumbed to Cancer but all of them will be improving their health and fitness along the way. One of the best things about the Race for Life is how it has captured the imagination of thousands of women and inspired them to train and get fit to complete the event.

For many women taking part, the race will be a completely new experience, having never run in an event or trained for a race in their lives. Having trained many women for the event, many of whom have never run a step before, it is fantastic to see how much they improve, progressing from a walking programme to running continuously for 45 minutes or more! Even better, they thoroughly enjoy the training and seeing their improvements and cannot believe the buzz that they get from running.

It is important to remember that for some people, running is unsuitable, perhaps if they have joint problems or suffer from diseases such as diabetes but equally, for a great many people, running can open the door to a whole new world of health and fitness benefits. So, with the Race for Life being so popular it is appropriate to look at how running can benefit your health and fitness which just might inspire you to hit the roads.

Benefits of regular running training

1. **Stronger heart.** Regular jogging or running exercises your heart; the most important muscle in your body. By ensuring that your heart is healthy, you are helping protect yourself from cardiovascular disease.

2. **Greater lung capacity.** Running makes you breathe harder and get slightly breathless. The extra oxygen you're your body demands makes your lungs more efficient so that you can deliver more oxygen with each breath.

3. **Easier weight management.** Unlike swimming, cycling or rowing, running requires you to support your own bodyweight all the time. This means that as a calorie burner, it is very hard to beat so keeping your weight in balance becomes much easier.

4. **Reduced cholesterol.** Regular cardiovascular (CV) exercise has been shown to reduce cholesterol levels. Reduced cholesterol levels are a further indicator of good CV health.

5. **Increased energy levels.** As a result of regular training, women are amazed at how much more energy they have for everyday tasks and how much easier those tasks have become.

6. **Lower body fat.** Sustained CV exercise is a fantastic calorie burner, gradually converting those unwanted pounds into energy, resulting in a lean, trim physique.

7. **Stronger legs.** Obviously leg muscles are the primary muscles used for running, which get significantly stronger as your training increases. Slim and toned legs are a further benefit.

8. **Improved self-esteem.** Simply put, when you're fit and healthy, you feel good about yourself!

All in all, a tremendous package of benefits from what is essentially an activity that needs little more than a good quality pair of running shoes.

Your great race

What you do in the final few days before a race can have a significant bearing on how you perform on the day and hence your final preparations are very important. The following dos and don'ts of race preparation are applicable to races of any distance and include workable tips to help you get the most out of your event:

The Dos and Don'ts of race preparation

- **Do . . . stick to tried and tested foods on the day**, so as not to risk upsetting your stomach. You may be travelling and be slightly nervous so to avoid problems, eat what you would normally eat and save any experimentation for your training runs.

- **Don't . . . wear new kit or shoes**. Particularly if you haven't previously broken them in during a training run. Occasionally, new trainers, shorts or vests can chafe and cause blisters and the last thing you want when you're trying to perform at your best is discomfort to distract your focus.

- **Do . . . back off your training in the final few days.** If you've been used to regularly churning out the miles, it can be difficult to break that habit and runners often fear that a missed day will mean that they lose fitness. In reality, a gradual taper will help your body bounce back after your training, so that you're primed for a great performance on race day.

- **Don't . . . set off too fast.** Probably the most common mistake that runners make is to surge away when the start gun fires, only to realise after a mile or so that they've set off too quickly and ruined their chances of running an even paced race. The key is to channel your adrenaline and excitement, keeping controlled through the early stages and equalising your effort across the whole distance.

- **Do . . . have a plan!** If you're hoping to optimise your performance you need to know what you want to achieve and what you need to do to achieve your personal goal. That means knowing what pace you intend to run and how you're going to approach your race. During the final few days, when you should have some more time because you're reducing your training volume, calculate your own personal race strategy so that when you line up, you're *'in the zone'* and ready to perform at your best.

- **Don't . . . arrive late!** Many good runners mess up their preparations by arriving late and then have to rush their warm-up so that they toe the start line less than focused, which impacts on their performance. Instead, look to arrive an hour before the race starts, which will give you ample time to warm-up, check-out the start and finish areas and generally prepare without hurrying.

- **Do . . . warm up.** Think of your body like a car engine – it runs much more efficiently when it's warm, so to correctly prepare for your race, you need to run the engine for a while. Begin with some light jogging for approximately 10 minutes, followed by mobility exercises and stretches for the legs, before taking up your position in the starting line-up a couple of minutes before the gun fires. That way you won't lose the benefits of your warm-up by standing around getting cold.

- **Don't . . . set yourself a single target.** Despite training correctly and paying attention to your race preparation, running a race can still be a bit of a hit and miss affair. There are many additional factors that can affect your performance, such as how you feel on the day, how challenging the course is and the weather conditions

– all of which are outside of your control. If you set a single target and external factors cause you to miss it, you will be extremely disappointed, whereas if you set yourself a range of goals, from 'getting round', to a specific time target, to an ultimate target, you are certain to take something away from your race whatever happens and you'll finish on a positive note.

SuperTip

Knowledge is power so they say and with respect to your race, knowledge of the course is key to your performance. To really prepare thoroughly, try and train over the course at least once, so that you have first-hand knowledge of any tough hills and twists and turns, so that come race day, you're not surprised by 'a cheeky little hill' that the organisers have subtly positioned in the final mile! Additionally, having run the course, you can enhance your preparation by mentally running over it in your mind during the preceding days – but make sure that you programme in a positive performance with you crossing the line in a great time and a smile on your face!

Smoking

> *'The best way to stop smoking is just to stop, no ifs, ands or butts'.*
> ***AMERICAN SOCIAL COMMENTATOR***

Time to quit?

With a ban on smoking in public places fully effective, whether you support the Government's drive to outlaw smoking or not, the initiative will certainly focus the UK's ten million smokers on the health issues surrounding their habit. With over 120,000 smoking related deaths annually, quitting warrants serious consideration and even if you've been a long-term or even a lifelong smoker, within 20 minutes of stopping, you will begin to enjoy health improvements! Furthermore, if you can maintain your focus and give up for ever, you make massive inroads on your likelihood of contracting smoking related diseases such as heart disease and lung cancer.

Consider the following countdown of health benefits from quitting:

Quitting smoking health benefits timeline

- **Within 20 minutes . . .** Giving up smoking brings almost instant health benefits and the longer you abstain, the greater they are. For example, every time you light up, your blood pressure and your heart rate increase but after just 20 minutes of stopping smoking, both these key measures of your health will return to normal levels.

- **Within 8 hours . . .** You're well into the process of clearing the accumulated toxins in your body and nicotine and carbon monoxide levels in your bloodstream reduce by 50%. Oxygen levels in your bloodstream will return to normal, improving your circulation such that the risk of you suffering a heart attack starts to fall.

- **Within 1 day . . .** The absence of a continual 'top-up' of the toxins contained in every cigarette results in carbon monoxide being completely eliminated from your body and your lungs will now begin to clear. You should now find that you're starting to breathe easier and the typical 'early morning coughing' that is so symptomatic of smoking reduces.

- **Within 2 days . . .** After just 48 hours, nicotine is eliminated from your body and you will notice that your sense of smell improves and that you can taste food better. Smoking blunts these key senses and ex smokers find that their improved ability to enjoy food is fantastic. Also, when you smoke, you experience a continual decline in lung function but after just two days that decline halts. You are now seriously back on the road to better health and recovery.

- **Within 3 days . . .** Although the idea of exercising may seem horrendous because you find that you get breathless with just the slightest exertion, just 72 hours after quitting, your lung capacity improves further, which will make exercising easier. This is a great time to carefully introduce some light cardiovascular exercise, which will accelerate the further elimination of smoking toxins and fast-track improvements to your lung function and circulatory system.

- **Within 1 month . . .** When you smoke, one of the most obvious damaging effects is an increase in wrinkles and a lack of colour in the face. However, after a month, your skin loses its greyish pallor and you will find fewer wrinkles when you check in the mirror.

- **Within 3 months . . .** After 3 months, you will be experiencing serious health benefits - most notably that your circulation improves. That means that your entire cardiovascular system is healthier, ie: your heart, lungs, arteries and veins and you are well out of the woods.

- **Within 9 months . . .** By now you will experience much less coughing and wheezing and your lung function will be more efficient. You are now seriously an ex-smoker and by combining regular exercise with your continued focus, not only will you get fitter but the health benefits listed in the timeline below will arrive earlier.

- **Within 1 year . . .** Approximately 33% of deaths caused by smoking are related to heart disease – that's 40,000 deaths annually, or one person dying every 15 minutes. However, if you have managed to quit for 12 months, you will have halved your risk of suffering heart disease, compared to a smoker.

- **Within 5 years . . .** Similarly, after five years of quitting, the benefits of stopping continue to rack up and you will have halved your risk of having a heart attack, compared to a smoker.

- **Within 10 years . . .** Lung cancer accounts for almost one quarter of all smoking related deaths but by your tenth anniversary of quitting, you will have halved your risk of developing lung cancer, compared to a smoker.

- **Within 15 years . . .** Forecasting 15 years in advance may seem like too far to look ahead but this statistic is hugely significant. Studies have shown that by the time you have given up for 15 years, your risk of suffering a heart attack falls to the same level as someone who has never smoked. That is a massive fact because it demonstrates that you can effectively 'turn back the clock' regarding your health and enjoy the same health benefits as a lifelong non-smoker if you are successful in giving up!

SuperTip

After just one year of giving up smoking, at today's prices, the average 20-a-day smoker will have saved several thousand pounds, which will buy you membership of a top quality gym for a year and two weeks holiday in the sun! Now there's an incentive!

10 steps to a smoke-free zone

Giving up smoking is very similar to embarking upon a fitness programme. It doesn't mater how old you are or for how long you've been smoking (or similarly neglecting your fitness), as soon as you stop smoking (or start exercising), you begin to enrich your life through improved health benefits, irrespective of your previous history.

So, if you're thinking about giving up smoking but need some focus and genuinely workable strategies that can help you stop, keep you motivated and finally break your habit, then follow the 10 steps to a smoke-free zone to help you change your life – for the better!

The 10 point plan to quitting smoking.

1. **Don't give up – yet!** Giving up smoking is a serious undertaking which needs planning and organisation so that you give yourself the best chance of success. So randomly deciding to give up on a whim is most likely to lead to failure. To begin with, continue with

your normal smoking routine for a week but keep a 'smoking diary' detailing where, when and how often you smoke. This will identify your personal smoking patterns and triggers, so that you can plan to replace them with alternative activities.

2. **Plan, plan, plan.** Most successful endeavours involve a plan and forward strategy and giving up smoking should be no different. Now that you know your personal smoking patterns, put together a personal action plan detailing how, when and why you'll be quitting. Will you need to change your routine to bypass smoking triggers? Will you need to bypass specific working or leisure patterns to keep you out of the smoking loop? How important is it to you to finally free yourself of cigarettes? What are your personal incentives? Are they financial, health related, domestic pressure or perhaps a combination? Write everything down and cover every base.

3. **Set a date for stopping.** To begin to put your plan into action, you now need to commit to a specific date when you're going to quit. Choose the most suitable day that gives you the best chance of success; possibly a weekend day without workplace smoking triggers or alternatively a low stress workday that fits in with your plan. When you've decided on D-Day, you then need to communicate it. Tell friends, family, work colleagues – as many people as possible so that they can both support you in your quest and also so that they can also help with your triggers – such as not offering you a cigarette, or the opportunity to smoke.

4. **Prepare.** With D-Day on the horizon you now need to finalise your preparations for giving up. The night before you stop, remove all traces of smoking from your life. Ashtrays, lighters, matches, cigarettes – everything goes into the bin – for good! Tomorrow you begin a new life, one without cigarettes, so go for it! Check over your personal quitting plan because tomorrow is a fresh start.

5. **STOP!** The day finally arrives and you enter your smoke-free existence. Put your anti-trigger strategies into effect immediately and refer to your commitment to quit as soon as you wake up to reinforce your resolve. Thereafter it's a just a normal day but with an extra special focus.

6. **Keep stopping!** The early hours and days are the hardest but it is also during this period when your motivation will be at its highest so when you feel the urge to smoke, really focus on your personal reasons for giving up and put yourself in situations where you cannot succumb to the temptation. Keep reminding yourself how

long you've given up for and refer back to the chronological list of health benefits that get more extensive for every hour that you remain smoke-free.

7. **Get active!** Distraction therapy can be really effective when you're challenged by the temptation to have another cigarette so keeping active is an excellent way of distracting yourself from smoking again. Boredom can easily lead to you focusing upon your desire to smoke so keep as busy as you can. Strategies can include exercise, tackling a DIY job that you've been putting off, throwing yourself into a work project, ploughing through the raft of domestic chores – in fact anything that fits with you and your plan.

8. **Clock milestones.** Every day and situation will bring new challenges so each time you overcome a smoking hurdle, record your achievement. Your first day at work without smoking, your first meal that you don't end with a cigarette, the first party where you avoided smoking and so on. All these milestones are success stories and by recording them you'll gradually build up a picture of your success as you progress towards your major goal.

9. **Reward yourself!** Remember, every hour leads to another day of success, which is another step closer to your overall goal, so when you win mini battles en route to winning the war, reward yourself. When a day becomes a week, weeks become a month and so on; buy yourself something with the savings that you've made from not spending money on cigarettes. Chart your progress and celebrate your achievements – it'll help keep you motivated.

10. ***'Just one'* WILL hurt!** Even though you may have abstained for days and weeks, you can still experience cravings and certain situations will test your resolve. This is the most difficult time – when you've given up for a while and your guard is potentially down. 'Just one' WILL hurt because it's the slippery slope to renewing your addiction, emptying your bank balance and putting you back after all your hard work. Keep your focus and walk away.

Training Smartly

> *'The difference between commitment and involvement? Think of ham and eggs: the chicken is involved but the pig is committed'.*
> ***Martina Navratilova***

Save time for exercise

The scourge of modern day living is that we never seem to have enough time – for anything. Despite more and more labour and time saving gadgets, from increased car ownership to internet shopping – all designed to save us time; we still seem short of it. Nowadays, our lifestyles are frequently a constant whirl of activities and we rush from one to the other, barely pausing for breath. One of the problems here is the lack of available time for that most important of activities for good all-round and long-term health – exercise. Very often it's exercise that gets sidelined in favour of other things because *'we're just too busy'*.

However, making time for exercise is important and aside from physiological benefits, your exercise sessions allow you some quality time for yourself, away from the demands of the phone, e-mail etc. Building regular exercise into your life is a strategy for life, so let's look at tips to help you integrate exercise into your life and keep that motivation going!

SuperTip

Does fitting 2 resistance training sessions, 3 cardiovascular sessions and some flexibility training into your week sound difficult? Well, there are 168 hours in a week and if you can commit to using just 3% of that available time for exercise, with a correctly structured fitness routine you could get into fantastic shape. For such a tiny percentage of your time, isn't that a commitment worth making?

Top tips for maintaining your exercise

1. **Make a date.** Make an arrangement with a friend to meet them at the gym or go walking / jogging together. Because you've made that commitment with someone else, there's less of a chance that you'll duck out of your exercise session, particularly as you've planned it into your day.

2. **Superset!** Super-setting is a great technique to save time in the gym. Used correctly, it can cut your exercise time by 50% - yet still give you the same results! Instead of having rest periods between two sets of an exercise, you select an alternative exercise which rests the muscle that you've just trained, but exercises the opposite one, before you complete that second set.

   Eg: Alternate exercises for chest and upper back, stomach and lower back, front and back of upper arm, front and back of thighs, etc.

3. **Exercise and commute.** With traffic congestion ever on the increase, by combining exercise with the morning or evening trip to work can not only save you a trip to the gym later but it can also save you commuting time.

   Eg: Walking or cycling as part of your commute is a healthy start to the day, or even jogging if there are washing facilities available at your workplace.

4. **Kick-start your day!** Not one for every day of the week, but occasionally, try setting the alarm clock a little earlier and pitching up early at the gym or swimming pool, or simply venturing outside for a walk or jog. It's a great start to your day and you'll be invigorated for hours afterwards.

5. **Miss the soaps!** People often say to me that they don't have time to workout but they are regular viewers of all the TV soap operas. Missing the odd couple of episodes doesn't kill the storylines and will free up an hour or two for you to fit in an exercise session.

6. **Maximise your weekend!** For many people, the weekend is a time away from the 9 to 5 and the opportunity to catch up on chores and have some family time. It can also be the time to fit some exercise into your life, either alone, with friends or perhaps with the family, where you all do an activity together like swimming.

7. **Goal!** There's nothing like setting yourself a goal to foster commitment to exercise. By having a target to aim for, your sessions have focus and purpose and you're more likely to factor exercise into your week as you work towards your goal. Your target could be anything from weight loss, to completing an event – providing that it's your choice and personal to you, so that you have some real buy-in to keep you focused.

8. **New, new, new!** Don't get stuck in a rut with the same old boring exercise routine that you've always done. As well as failing to get results, your motivation will suffer and you'll easily find an excuse not to workout and then you'll do something else. Why not step outside of your comfort zone and try a new activity, exercise class or experience. Take out a trial membership at a new gym, learn a new sport, join a club or get some professional coaching to introduce you to different training techniques. Something new will revitalise you and reawaken your enthusiasm again – so you'll want to make time to workout.

Train even smarter

A key element of your fitness jigsaw is to focus on a target. After a few weeks of training, if your programme lacks variety or you aren't achieving quite the results that you hoped for, it is common to lose some motivation. One way forward is to set a series of goals. Your goals can be absolutely anything, providing that they are YOUR goals and have meaning for YOU. To get you thinking, the most popular goals are losing weight, dropping a dress size, improving flexibility, toning up and improving your posture. Your goals could be anything that is relevant to you and your health and fitness programme.

The best goals are ones that you can continuously monitor to check your progress. For example, if weight loss is your target, then aiming to lose 1 - 1½ pounds per week is an ideal short-term target, with an end goal of perhaps losing a specific amount in three months. Along the way you are likely to find that you've dropped a dress size/waist size as well – a further measure of your progress.

So, to keep your motivation going, follow the smartTRAINING goal setting system and keep your focus.

How to set smartTRAINING goals

Firstly, take a little time out with a pen and paper and sit down to think through exactly what you are trying to achieve from your health and fitness programme. Write these ideas down. Then, check that your goals follow the smartTRAINING system below:

- **S – Specific.** Your goals need to be specific and relevant to you and should state exactly what needs to be done.
- **M – Measurable.** You should be able to monitor your progress week-on-week and identify when you finally hit your target.
- **A – Achievable.** Your goal should be within your capabilities to achieve.
- **R – Realistic.** Your goal must be realistic, factoring in available resources such as time etc.
- **T – Time-based.** It is important to set a clear date for achieving your goal.

Consider the following two goals:

1. **Goal A**: I want to lose weight.
2. **Goal B**: I want to lose 1 – 1½ pounds a week totalling ¾ of a stone in time for my holiday at Easter.

- **Goal A** is vague, non-specific, has no week-on-week monitoring system, may or may not be achievable and has no end target. Hence Goal A is a poor goal.
- **Goal B** however is very specific, measurable week by week as the target day approaches, is both realistic and achievable in line with correct weight loss recommendations and has a time target: Easter. Goal B is an excellent goal.

Your motivation will fluctuate and many other commitments will rear their head over the coming weeks and months but by creating your own personal smartTRAINING goals, you can really put focus into your health and fitness plan and help maintain your motivation when you're tempted to back off. Regularly check on whether you're achieving your targets so that you don't lose interest. Little stepping stones such as losing a pound in weight each week will help keep you working towards your ultimate target.

The TRUTH about Fitness . . .

> *'Fitness is good for you – no one can argue with that'* **MIKE SEARLE**

Fitness truths

Fitness issues are extremely emotive subjects and hardly a day goes by in the media without a celebrity endorsing an 'amazing new diet' or a story focuses on some nugget of health and fitness information that misrepresents key facts. In our 'information age', there can often be 'too much information' presented incorrectly and with such a mismatch of data, it can sometimes be difficult to separate fact from fiction. The focus should always be on plain-speaking facts – backed up by real-life examples so as not to muddle the issue and so on that theme, I am trying to lay to rest some of the common myths about fitness, setting the record straight with the TRUTH about Fitness!

TRUE fitness facts

1. **Rest, rest, rest.** The most important component of your fitness programme is . . . rest. Many people believe that a day where you don't train is a day wasted and your rivals will be stealing a march on you. Well actually, if you don't factor in rest and recovery, your rivals will steal a march on you because you'll either end up suffering from over-training syndrome, (which at best will lead to impaired performances), your immune system will be depressed and you'll pick up an illness or you'll end up injured.

2. **Resistance training for all.** Men, women, young and old alike, everyone will benefit from working out with weights to maintain muscle mass and strength and also to maintain good posture. No, women won't end up looking like Popeye but they will enjoy lean, toned bodies which will also support their weight management efforts because their improved musculature will burn more calories, day in, day out. Lifting weights is of particular importance in our increasingly labour-saving world because only a generation ago, our lives required far more physical activity – which provided numerous health and fitness benefits but nowadays 21st century living is unfortunately frequently lacking in exercise.

3. **Diets don't work.** I'll repeat that statement; DIETS DON'T WORK. If I had a pound for each diet that I'd seen people suffering with and failing to get results with, I could retire! Our bodies are

designed to be active on a daily basis and eat as broad a range of unprocessed foods as possible in order to provide a correctly balanced nutrition programme. The practice of denying your body essential nutrition in an attempt to achieve weight loss is fuelled by 'lifestyle' television programmes and glossy magazines that is always doomed to failure. However, adopting a whole-food, natural nutrition regime, combined with exercise continuity is the healthy and sustainable route to effective weight management.

4. **Boring, boring, boring.** We frequently hear that exercise is boring. Well, I have to agree . . . almost; exercise can be boring – if you let it. If you continually vary the exercise stimulus in the form of location and the types of exercise that you do, your workouts will never be boring. In fact it's a proven fact that exercise can be addictive – the 'runner's high' is a good example of that, where runners (or anyone indulging in cardiovascular exercise) can experience a real and genuine feel-good factor both during and after a session, due to chemicals called endorphins being released by the brain that have been proven to improve your mood. Of course if exercise can become addictive then it must be enjoyable!

5. **Flexibility = longevity.** It's not challenging or tough, it doesn't take long, it's relaxing, it helps prevent injury, it improves mobility and performance, yet most people ignore it. I'm talking about flexibility training, probably the easiest component of fitness to maintain. In fact you can even do it in your front room whilst watching TV! If you want to enjoy the benefits of your exercise programme long-term, without compromising your movement, technique or suffering an injury – then ten minutes stretching after each exercise session is a great way to chill out and will also help bring you longevity in your chosen exercise discipline.

The 'best' exercise . . ?

Hardly a day goes by without someone whom I meet asking me what is *'the best exercise'*. Now of course that's a very open question and it is sometime qualified with a sentence or two such as:

1. '. . . for toning my legs'
2. '. . . for losing weight'
3. '. . . for my heart'
4. ' . . .to build up my chest'

and so on.

Well of course there is no 'one size fits all' answer because in recommending a *'best exercise'*, your age, current fitness, training time, possible medical conditions, previous exercise background and a whole myriad of other factors need to be considered. Hence, I often end up asking a whole raft of questions in return myself before providing the correct answer!

However, the entire concept of *'the best exercise'* does stimulate considerable interest so let's look at a range of common fitness targets and a selection of exercise ideas that are very effective at achieving those goals.

The 'best' exercise for . . .

1. **Losing weight.** This is probably the most common question because weight loss is the number one target for a great many people. There are numerous exercise strategies for losing weight, with aerobic exercise top of the charts – of which there are similarly numerous options. Cycling, swimming, aerobics classes, dancing, circuit training, walking, jogging, running, rowing, gym machines are just a few ideas – all of which will work. However, the number one choice is the exercise which you prefer the most because that is the one that you're most likely to continue with long-term. Taking that a stage further, any sort of exercise where you support your own bodyweight will burn more calories than one where your weight is supported. So for example, running is a bigger calorie burner than swimming. Additionally, working out with weights to build muscle will further support weight loss because muscle burns more calories than other tissues.

2. **Toning the stomach.** This is another key target area for many people and is one which needs a multiple attack strategy to be really effective. Whilst sit-up type exercises will strengthen the stomach muscles, frequently they need to be carried out with exercises for the lower back to maintain the body in correct balance. This should be assessed prior to you starting to exercise. Additionally, core exercises which target your deep abdominal postural muscles will help improve your posture and also 'pull everything in' around the waist and are a key part of the equation. Finally, maintaining a suitable bodyweight will ensure that excess fat doesn't accumulate around your midriff and will help to give you that flat, toned look.

3. **Toning the upper arms.** 'Bingo wings', the name that many women use to refer to un-toned upper arms are dreaded by women everywhere and I am often asked how to sculpt the underside of the upper arm to make it look more attractive. The

solution is two-fold; firstly, exercise the muscles in that area (triceps) and secondly, ensure that overall, your bodyweight is correct so that excess body-fat isn't carried there. Remember though, whilst an exercise can focus on a specific body part, these exercises should be incorporated into an all over and all-round exercise programme so that you get total body, long-term health and fitness benefits.

4. **Keeping your heart healthy.** CV exercise for your heart and lungs is essential for all round health and fitness and if you do nothing else, this is the most important area to target. If your engine isn't running well, it doesn't matter how good the bodywork is, you'll soon grind to a halt. So aim for exercise that you do continuously for at least 30 minutes for several times per week that gets you breathless. Any of the exercises listed for losing weight above are suitable, just ensure that you are getting breathless and not 'going through the motions'. Make sure that your exercise time counts and you are really getting a valuable workout.

5. **Building muscle.** If you are looking to improve your strength and improve your physique then you need to commit to building up your condition in the gym by resistance training. Initially you should focus upon introducing your body to weight training using light weights and perfecting your technique. Later, you can then start to lift heavier weights and if time permits, separate your workouts into specific muscle groups that you target repeatedly to enable them to adapt and grow larger. Hence there is no single 'best exercise' for muscle building, rather a wide range of exercises to continually challenge your body to adapt to different training loads. Finally, don't neglect cardiovascular training, to keep your heart healthy and also to ensure that your body composition is optimal and you get the visual muscle definition that you're aiming for.

SuperTip

Exercise keeps your brain fit too! As well as the physical benefits of exercise, recent Swedish research has found that regular cardiovascular exercise during midlife, guards against Alzheimer's disease. The Swedish study followed 1,500 men and women and found that those who were physically active in their late 40's and early 50's could reduce their risk of dementia by 50% - which is another great reason to get active.

Fitness myths exploded!

The world of health and fitness is awash with half truths and untruths – frequently centred on the popular theme of weight loss and hardly a day goes by without some form of fitness misrepresentation being repeated in the media.

So it's time to put the record straight and dispel the more popular myths surrounding health and fitness, together with the REAL truth that hopefully will put these myths to bed for good!

Super 7 health & fitness myths

- **Myth No. 1: Muscle turns to fat when you stop exercising.** This is as good a place to begin as any because it's completely false. Muscle and fat are two completely different tissue types and there is absolutely no way that one can magically change into the other – it's impossible! However, what can happen is that if you stop exercising, you can experience muscle wastage, where your muscle mass reduces in size and then if that is combined with excess weight gain in the form of body fat then it can appear that you've traded muscle for fat. The solution is to maintain your levels of activity to ensure that you don't suffer from muscle wastage, in other words – keep it going!

- **Myth No. 2: I'm too old to exercise.** Complete rubbish! Countless studies have proved that a correctly structured exercise programme will make a huge difference to the quality of your life, irrespective of either your age or when you start working out. In fact, a very recent study found that exercise not only slows down but actually reverses the aging process which is fantastic news. The solution is to banish any age-related thoughts and take those steps to improving the quality of your life – as soon as possible!

- **Myth No. 3: If you're overweight you should avoid exercise.** I can understand where this myth is coming from because the ethos here is that anyone who's overweight, could potentially injure themselves whilst exercising or alternatively, it's dangerous for someone who's unfit to begin working out. However, someone who is either overweight, unfit or both is exactly the person who should be starting to train – or else the consequences could be disastrous. There is a proviso here and that is that anyone in these categories needs professional support and guidance for their safety but as to avoiding exercise – ridiculous!

- **Myth No. 4: Miracle machines and supplements fast-track your fitness.** Sadly, this one too is a no-no. Rapid weight loss tablets or powders, often containing a *'special magic ingredient'* and retailing at an exorbitant price, are at best a waste of money and at worst, a positive danger to your health. Similarly, miracle pieces of equipment that promise amazing results in an unbelievably minimal time are never the fantastic fitness solution that the manufacturers claim and cannot replace correct training, executed correctly and structured for you and your personal goals. The best advice is to ditch the miracle 'solutions' and invest your time and effort more wisely!

- **Myth No. 5: You can spot reduce fat.** Unfortunately, no, you cannot target a specific area for weight loss such as the underside of the upper arms or the waist because your genetics and body type determine where you predominantly store fat and how you'll lose it. What you can do is to target a specific muscle or muscle groups to increase your muscle tone in a particular area and combine that with aerobic exercise to reduce your overall level of body fat. You will then achieve the slimmer and toned look that you desire.

- **Myth No. 6: Skipping meals helps you lose weight.** Oh no, definitely not! When you miss meals in an attempt to reduce your calorie intake, your metabolic rate (the speed at which you burn calories) slows and you increase the likelihood that you'll go for an eating binge later on. That binge is further compounded by the fact that because your body is desperate for fuel, you'll seek out the high fat and sugar foods that contain predominantly empty calories with minimal nutritional value which will then increase your weight gain – exactly the opposite of what you're attempting to achieve. Following a balanced nutrition plan of non-processed foods is the only way forward for both healthy eating and to support your weight management.

- **Myth No. 7: Exercise is not necessary for weight loss.** Well, there is a grain of truth in this myth – as there typically is in the best myths. By reducing your calorie intake, you can lose weight – up to a point. However, what happens is that very rapidly, your body recognises that it's in 'starvation mode' and lowers your metabolic rate to conserve fuel. This results in a cessation of weight loss which leads you to ditch the diet, resume your previous eating plan and gain weight again. However, if you sensibly combine healthy eating with regular exercise, you can easily double your calorie burn and that keeps you healthy, not just slim – a very important difference.

Walking

> *'Does the road wind uphill all the way? Yes, to the very end'.*
> ***WALTER DE LA MERE***

Walk the walk

When was the last time that you walked a mile or more? Nowadays the car is king and many people walk just a few steps to their car in the morning, drive to work and then walk a few steps into their workplace, sitting down for much of their day. And that's it. Walking brings a whole stack of health and fitness benefits, costs nothing and if you're a little self conscious about beginning an exercise programme; no-one need know that you're actually working out!

Considering that walking has to be the cheapest, most accessible and easiest form of exercise available and is achievable by almost everyone at their own personal level, we should all be walking more, from toddlers to pensioners because the benefits are so great.

Read on for the top ten benefits from walking which might just tempt you to stride out and - *walk the walk!*

Top 10 walking fitness tips & benefits

1. **Walk briskly.** Rather than casually strolling along, maximise your walking fitness gains by striding out and walking fast. If you double your walking pace, in addition to getting greater fitness benefits, you'll burn twice as many calories in the same time – which has to be a winner.

2. **Target 30 minutes.** For your walking workout, aim to walk non-stop for a minimum of 30 minutes at a time. If 30 minutes is difficult at first, then build up gradually to 30 minutes and increase from there.

3. **Keep a walking diary.** Your walking diary is personal to you and a log of every walk you complete. Inside, detail the distance covered (or time your walk took if you're not sure of the distance), how you felt and any other information that you want to include. As you progress, you'll be able to look back on your early sessions and see how your fitness has improved – which is an excellent motivational tool.

4. **Pound those pounds!** Walking is a great calorie burner so if you want to shift a few inches (permanently so that they won't return), walking is your friend. A short 45 minute walk each day can burn up to 300 calories which equates to 2½ pounds of body-fat lost each month – without any dietary changes! So forget about calorie restricting fad diets that don't work and focus on the health *giving* benefits of walking instead!

5. **Aiding digestion.** A regular walk will help speed the passage of food through your body so that abdominal and bowel discomfort becomes a thing of the past. Many people suffer terribly by being unable to keep their digestive system regular but in line with good nutritional practices, if you build walking into your day, digestive problems should be a thing of the past. Furthermore, studies have shown that regular walking can reduce incidence of bowel cancer by up to 40%.

6. **When to walk the walk.** That's the beauty of walking, you can do it all the time and combine it with other activities too. Taking the kids to and from school, talking on the phone, collecting your local newspaper, running short errands, visiting friends, breaking out of the office at lunchtime – the opportunities are endless!

7. **All round health.** In addition to strengthening the heart and associated CV system, walking builds strength in the legs, improves coordination and also makes you feel good – similar to the runner's high that runners are known to experience.

8. **Walking offsets osteoporosis.** Brittle bone disease or osteoporosis is endemic with NHS costs for treating the disease estimated at close to £1 billion annually. One of the most common fracture sites is the hip but walking is a great way to strengthen the lower skeleton. Half of all women will be affected by osteoporosis at some time in their lives, with 25% over the age of 60 suffering a fracture, so regular walking guards against this awful disease.

9. **Stress busting.** Any CV exercise is good for combating stress - the 21st century malaise and walking fits the bill perfectly. Simply breaking out of the office, telephone, e-mail environment for even a short walk will leave you refreshed and ready to go again. Your circulation gets a boost, you loosen up, have time to think away from distractions and you never know, by the time you return invigorated, you might just get that Eureka moment that puts everything in place!

10. **Walking further.** Once you've got the walking bug, the opportunities are limitless. From local walking groups to the Ramblers Association, getting out and exploring the open countryside is healthy and extremely enjoyable. The UK is blessed with some fantastic walking country and long distance footpaths such as Offa's Dyke and the South Downs Way to perhaps a more serious challenge, climbing Scafell Pike, Ben Nevis and Snowden, the highest peaks in England, Scotland and Wales.

SuperTip

It's a fact: walking makes you healthier by boosting your immune system. Intense exercise can actually damage your immune system and make you more open to illness and infection – elite athletes are a good example because they frequently come down with colds and viral infections. However, walking, which is at a lower intensity has proven immune system boosting properties, effectively increasing the proportion of the cells that fight bacteria and viruses. Another good reason to walk the walk!

Warming Up & Cooling Down

'Fail to prepare, prepare to fail'. **BENJAMIN FRANKLIN**

Prepare to exercise . . .

Whether it is cooking, fixing the car, DIY, gardening or any activity, preparation is extremely important and preparation for exercise is no different. Whether an exercise session is in a warm gym, outdoors, or at home, correct preparation is essential. Many people simply launch straight into an intensive session without any form of introduction to the demands that they are placing on their bodies, which is an extremely risky practice. If your preparation is inadequate, at the very least you are limiting the benefits from your session but more importantly, insufficient preparation significantly increases your risk of injury.

The sort of pre-exercise preparation that's necessary is a thorough warm-up that fully sets up your body for your chosen activity. At elite level, a top athlete may warm-up for well over an hour, raising their body temperature, mobilising joints, stretching and carrying out specific routines that replicate the movements in their sport. For most of us, this is both unnecessary and impractical. By the time we had completed a warm-up of this length it would be time to get changed again! However, we can still carry out a useful and important pre-exercise routine at the beginning of every session, which is an activity specific warm-up.

A warm-up serves a great many purposes. To begin with, it raises your body temperature and heart rate, which increases blood supply to the working muscles. Because your muscles are warm and well supplied with blood, they are then primed for action and they also relax and stretch much more easily. It is equally important to ensure that you have a full range of movement, so by also incorporating mobility exercises into your warm-up, by carefully putting each joint through its full range of movement, you fully lubricate the joints, making their movements more efficient.

So how should you incorporate a warm-up into your exercise routine? Your warm-up should be progressive, starting very easily and gradually building up but never at an extremely intense level. You don't want to warm up so intensely that you are too fatigued for your main session! Some form of light cardiovascular exercise such as walking, jogging or utilising a piece of gym equipment like the cross-trainer or rowing machine is ideal and should take a minimum of 5 minutes.

Immediately following this CV exercise, you should loosen up the shoulders, elbows, spine, pelvis, knees and ankles by gradually putting your arms and legs through their full range of movement. This will be easier than when you started because your CV warm-up will have helped loosen up the working muscles.

Next you might want to carry out a few specific warm-up drills. For example, if your main session is weight-lifting, you could incorporate some light resistance work, using the exact movements that you will use when you progress to heavier weights. Alternatively a badminton player might practice a range of shots around the court but at a slightly lower intensity than their forthcoming match.

Finally, begin your main session immediately following your warm-up, so you don't lose any of the benefits that the warm-up period has given you.

SuperTip

Before your next exercise session, spend a few minutes planning your warm-up to include light CV, mobility and also some movements that replicate the demands of your sport. The challenge is to keep it at less than 10 minutes! It will soon become part of your normal exercise routine and you will enjoy the benefits of a better session and reduce your risk of injury into the bargain!

Time to chill out . . .

At the end of your training session is the equally important cool-down. Whether it is a gym workout, a competitive match, or outdoor training - whatever type of exercise you are involved in, a cooling down period at the end is extremely important. As a comparison, if you prepare a meal in the kitchen, afterwards you have to tidy up and wash the dishes, so that everything is ready to be used again for the next meal. Your cool-down is just the same, it tidies everything up so that you are prepared for your next session. Your body is then better equipped for the next day or your next bout of training.

For example: elite cyclists will cool down for over an hour at the end of a day in the Tour de France but thankfully for most of us, a cool-down of that length is unnecessary! Your cool-down need only take a few minutes but should be an integral part of your session. Dispensing with a cool-down can result in muscle soreness the following day and will also negate many of the positive psychological benefits that are gained from your workout. From a psychological point of view, a gradual cooling down period facilitates relaxation as the more intense element of the training session has been completed. The primary physiological benefits that you can gain from a cool-down are the elimination of the by-products of exercise such as lactic acid (which can produce post-exercise muscle soreness) and the gradual return of blood pressure, heart rate and all the body's systems to their pre-exercise state.

So what sort of exercises should you do for your cool-down and how long should it take? The most important factor is to exercise during your cool-down at a much lower intensity than your main session. The idea is to gently stimulate blood flow around the body to eliminate any waste products, not add to your previous workout. A good idea is to do the same sort of exercise as your earlier training and utilising the same muscle groups, so that using the washing up analogy, you are 'tidying-up' the exact same muscles that have been worked. For example, if you have been running, then spend a few minutes doing some light jogging or walking. A spinning class should allow time for slowly turning the legs over with the resistance set very low and a good circuit training class would include some time jogging and walking around the sports hall, also combining light, rhythmical limb movements to disperse waste products. A key point to remember is that the more intense your session, the longer the cooling down period needs to be but generally, five to ten minutes is usually sufficient.

Finally, the chill out period of the cool-down is the ideal time for some mental training, recapping on how your workout went, whether you improved – or not and also provides a suitable opportunity to plan your next session and what you intend to get out of it

SuperTip

Apart from mobility exercises, avoid flexibility training before your workout and instead use your cool-down to do some stretching. After your main session, your mind and body will be relaxed, making conditions for stretching ideal because your muscles are thoroughly warmed up and any mental and physical tension has been eliminated. Hence, carrying out a few minutes flexibility training during your cool-down is the optimum time to maintain and also improve your flexibility.

Weather

> *'It is almost impossible to be fit and fearless without some sweating exercise most days'.*
>
> ***PERCY CERUTTY, RENOWNED ATHLETICS COACH***

Beat the heat

When summer arrives, we can look forward to clear skies, sunny days and rising temperatures. Good weather always puts a shine on things but a heat-wave can be quite a different matter, particularly if you're regularly exercising. Combating dehydration is a daily challenge for most people in normal conditions, but when the temperature rises, it can have a serious impact on your training and competing performances. As you dehydrate, your blood volume reduces and hence your heart has to work harder.

However there are many tools that you can use to keep your fluid levels topped up and still continue exercising so check out the following strategies that will enable you to maintain your fitness levels whilst the mercury rises.

Warm weather workout tips

1. **Before, during and after.** Hydration is one of the most neglected training strategies. By the time you feel thirsty, you're already dehydrated, so follow the *'little and often'* drinking rule throughout the day and prior to your workout, make sure that you have a long drink. During your session, (whether you're in the gym or outdoors), always carry a small water bottle with you and sip regularly. If you're out running, stash a water bottle in your garden and try doing a repeated loop course, passing your front gate several times. Each time you pass, briefly stop and take a drink. Post workout, drink as soon as possible to replace losses from sweating and continue in the same way for the rest of the day.

2. **Watch the clock!** Avoid exercising during the hottest part of the day and instead, try an early morning or late evening session when the temperatures are lower. A brisk session before work will not only beat the heat but will also set you up for the day ahead. Alternatively a later session can free you up for tasks during the day.

3. **Get kitted out.** Technology reigns supreme everywhere these days and training kit has benefited tremendously. Gone are the days of heavy, sweat absorbing, clammy, chafing t-shirts because now there's a huge range of hi-tech garments that will help keep you cool and more comfortable whilst you exercise. When buying kit, look for wicking fabrics that transport moisture rapidly away from the skin so that it evaporates fast, rather than old-fashioned cotton-type fabrics which are cheaper but will leave you feeling that you've been exercising in a hot, rough, wet bag! Mesh garments are also useful as they allow air to flow through them and to further help you keep cool, look for some of the newer fabrics that are specifically designed to stand proud of the body, allowing air to circulate and hence keep you cooler.

4. **Slow down!** Despite taking all these precautions, you're still going to get hot, so whilst the temperatures are high, modify your sessions slightly. In the gym, take longer recoveries and if you're training outside, reduce your pace and the intensity, particularly if you're planning a long, endurance-type session. You'll still be getting useful training in but by backing off a little, you'll be able to complete your whole session without problems.

5. **Try an alternative.** If the temperature gets too much then why not change your exercise routine? Seek out an air conditioned gym for your workout, go swimming instead of cycling in the heat or change your running route to a wooded area where you'll get more shade. With a little ingenuity and forward planning you can still keep fit and the change of scene might just invigorate your usual schedule!

6. **Avoid diuretics.** Caffeinated drinks such as tea, coffee, colas and alcohol all contribute to dehydration so during hot conditions, avoid or limit them as much as possible. Drinking a pint of a drink that is a diuretic will result in more than a pint of fluid being excreted by the body – contributing to dehydration. Instead, focus on consuming drinks such as plain water, squash and fruit juices.

Weight Management

> *'You are what you eat'.*
>
> **LUDWIG FEUERBACH, 19TH CENTURY FRENCH PHILOSOPHER**

Weighty issues

With low levels of activity and unsuitable food choices, being overweight and even obese is increasingly prevalent these days and for all-round good health and vitality it is vitally important not to be overweight. However, it appears that in many respects, the pendulum has swung completely in the opposite direction and so many people are now obsessed with losing weight and dieting, over and above the primary need to follow a healthy lifestyle, fitness programme and nutrition plan. Everywhere we go we are bombarded with television images, advertisements, media descriptions and signals about weight loss, suggesting that weight loss should be our sole aim. This is totally contrary to good health.

For example, there are many women who have spent years and years dieting in an effort to remain slim. At first glance they appear slim but actually, they're not slim, they're thin – which is entirely different. Through continual dieting, they have gradually stripped out muscle as well as body fat with the result that their bodies are weak, they have poor posture and they are setting themselves up for a multitude of functional problems as they age. This 'weight-loss focus' problem is perpetuated and compounded by the many 'slimming clubs' who weigh members each week, reinforcing the false message that the sole criteria should be targeting a specific weight rather than advocating a balanced healthy lifestyle encompassing a whole-food, non-processed nutrition plan coupled with an exercise programme that is tailored to their needs and goals.

The other common difficulty that people find when they embark on a dieting regime is that it doesn't work. The diet seems effective for a short period of time with noticeable weight loss in the early stages but the diet then becomes increasingly harder to maintain. This is commonly because the weekly weight loss is too great. Any diet that results in losing more than one to two pounds per week will cause lean muscle tissue as well as body fat to be lost. When the diet is abandoned and the original eating plan is resumed, the body reacts to the 'famine' diet and stores a greater percentage of calories as fat, effectively as an insurance policy against future diets. Additionally, the loss of lean muscle causes the body's constant calorie burner – your metabolic rate, to slow, so that your body actually require fewer calories than before you dieted. By resuming your original eating plan, you can end up eating more calories than you can burn, which in turn are stored as excess body fat.

So is there a solution to the common problem of weight management? The answer is yes. By adopting a whole-food, non-processed nutrition plan and balancing that plan with increased levels of activity and regular training. Exercise burns more calories and over time, even small changes such as walking short distances will make a difference to your calorie burn and will also initiate fitness improvements, all contributing to sustainable, long-term weight management in conjunction with a balanced healthy lifestyle, without the need for continual self-denial via an unpleasant 'diet'.

SuperTip

If you are struggling with your weight and have tried (unsuccessfully) many different diets, why not try this two-step weight management plan.

Step 1: Start a daily walking programme, trying to increase your total weekly mileage every other week as your fitness builds.

Step 2: Reduce your intake of processed and packet foods, replacing them with whole-food alternatives such as fruit.

I can guarantee that you won't lose half a stone in the first week but you will gradually lose weight and importantly, improve your fitness at the same time - the ideal, sustainable, weight-loss strategy.

Change your shape - easily

When you are monitoring weight loss, between one and one and a half pounds per week is the ideal rate. Lose weight faster than this and you will be hungry, you will be depriving your body of the correct nutrition that it needs and your weight-loss plan will fail in the long term. Also, by incorporating regular exercise into your life, you will tone up your muscles – which are heavier than fat, so using weight as an indicator can be false.

The real test of your regime is how you feel and look, not what the scales say.

Seven tips for burning more calories and changing your shape!

1. **Walk on, walk on.** Every mile you walk burns approximately 100 calories. A brisk lunchtime stroll for half an hour, combined with 10 minutes extra walking to and from work each day, five days a week, burns the equivalent of ½ a pound of fat a week, which equals a whopping 86,000 extra calories a year! Additionally, it exercises your heart, lungs and tones up your legs too.

2. **Worth the weight.** Muscle is a tremendous calorie burner. The energy 'cost' of carrying muscle is greater than body fat. Therefore, if you have two 10 stone people who do the same tasks each day, the one with toned muscles will burn more calories. Building more muscle will boost your metabolism, allowing you to burn up to an extra 200 calories a day. That equates to nearly another ½ pound of body fat each week.

3. **Core, core, core!** Core exercises are top of the charts for 'pulling everything in' around your abdomen. Try sitting on an exercise ball instead of a chair and you will find that you have to use your core muscles to help keep upright and balance. Before long you will be stronger and more toned and your new core muscles will help give you a new shape.

4. **Be an early bird.** An exercise session increases your metabolic rate, the speed at which your body burns calories. This rise can last for up to 15 hours, so a morning workout not only kick-starts your day, it also helps you burn more calories all day too!

5. **Stand up.** It's easy to spend a lot of our time sitting down. Watching TV, working at a computer, driving; so many of our daily activities are sedentary, so it's no surprise that we struggle to burn calories. To combat the problem, do more activities standing up. A classic example is holding a meeting in a room without chairs. You'll be amazed at how much quicker the meeting goes, no-one will want to drag it out, and they'll all want to hurry back to their desks for a rest! That's not including the extra calorie burning benefits!

6. **Try interval training.** Studies have shown that training more intensely for half an hour is more effective at burning calories than exercising at a much lower intensity for a whole hour. To get these benefits, simply alternate bursts of harder efforts with recovery periods. A good start point is one minute harder, two minutes easy. You could try walking, cycling, jogging, swimming or a cardiovascular machine form the gym.

Why not walk briskly for one minute, followed by two minutes of strolling. An additional benefit is that the time will fly past, particularly as your exercise session is only half as long!

7. **Get family active.** Children always enjoy a family activity – and from my experience, the more active the better! At weekends, try taking the family out for a walk, a cycle ride, a game of football, in fact anything that is active, family based and will burn more calories. By choosing a fun activity, you won't even notice that you're using more energy, which all contributes to your extra calorie burn.

SuperTip

Have fun! It's easy to get hung up about weight, calories, body shape etc and forget about enjoyment. Try to keep everything in balance and whichever shape changing tips you use, choose ones that you personally enjoy. That way, you'll continue with your exercise beyond a couple of weeks and reap the fantastic all-round health and fitness benefits long-term.

A shocking statistic

Here is one of the most shocking statistics of all. It concerns the disparity between the haves and have nots in that most basic of commodities – food. For the first time on record, the number of overweight people in the world outnumbers the number of malnourished. It is estimated that there are approximately 800 million people who do not have enough to eat but this figure is dwarfed by those who are overweight which now totals one billion people. Furthermore, of those one billion overweight people, an estimated 300 million are obese and if you are obese, approximately 30% or more of your bodyweight is fat.

The World Health Organisation describes obesity as *'one of the greatest public health challenges of the 21st century'* and without doubt, we are facing an increasingly grave problem. When you consider that in the UK, obesity levels have tripled in the past 20 years and an estimated 39%

of people are overweight, it is appropriate to identify tips and suggestions to help keep the flab at bay.

Super six tips to avoid unwanted weight gain

1. **Aim for 5-a-week.** We've all heard of the Government's 5-a-day campaign to encourage everyone to eat five portions of fruit and vegetables each day, well that should also be translated to exercise for a '5-a-week' campaign. Exercising at least five times a week, every week is the target, ideally for a minimum of 30 minutes each time. Remember that your exercise needs to be sufficiently intensive for you to get breathless but get a check-up with your GP before you start if you've not exercised for some time and also get professional guidance to ensure that you exercise safely and correctly, to maximise your training benefits.

2. **When you're not exercising – exercise!** In addition to your 5-a-week exercise sessions, try and introduce more activity into your everyday life. Try building more exercise into your daily activities from walking to standing to gardening or even DIY. When it comes to calorie burning, every little helps so in addition to careful, structured exercise, get active as often as possible.

3. **Target 10% fat.** Finding out what's in the food we eat these days is easy because every product has a wealth of nutritional information printed on the packet. However, food manufacturers can sometimes try to disguise or make it confusing to identify the exact nutritional breakdown. So when scanning labels, look for the column that is headed up 'per 100g' and try to eliminate products with a fat content that exceeds 10 grams – which is 10%.

4. **Target a target.** There's nothing like a target to put some focus into your weight loss programme and to make your target meaningful, write it down and display it in a prominent position so that you have a constant reminder of your goal. For weight loss to be sustainable and to avoid regaining the weight a few months later, don't try to lose more than 1½ - 2 pounds per week.

5. **Don't diet.** It seems as if almost the whole world is on a diet and you know, if diets of any description were even the slightest bit effective, the diet industry would soon go out of business. To quote the British Dietetic Association; *'a third of people end up heavier than their original weight after trying to diet for just a few weeks'.* The bottom line, is that diets don't work but healthy eating does. Ditch the high fat, high sugar, calorie laden processed food

choices, swapping them for simple, unadulterated fresh produce and support your healthy eating with as much exercise as possible – and you'll lose weight.

6. **Make breakfast a habit.** The word breakfast means *'breaking your fast'* because for the eight hours you've been sleeping, your body has been fasting and when you wake up, your fuel tank is not topped up. Omit breakfast and by mid-morning the munchies will have descended and before you know it, you'll be tempted to get a quick, hi calorie, short-term energy hit, such as a chocolate bar. Start the day with a simple and quick to make bowl of porridge or muesli and that temptation will not occur and you'll be revved up with more energy into the bargain!

Burn off the fat – fast!

Health and exercise researchers in Australia have discovered that a cardiovascular workout that intersperses intense bursts of exercise with light recoveries, burns more fat than someone who exercises for a similar period of time but at a continuous, steady pace. There has long been a view that if you want to burn fat then you should exercise at low intensities for prolonged periods of time but I have always challenged that theory. Yes, low intensity exercise is a fat burner and higher intensity exercise can burn more carbohydrate as fuel but equally it always appears to be overlooked that a higher intensity workout burns more calories overall. Hence if the intensity levels are selected correctly, because more calories are burnt overall with the more challenging workout, there can be a greater fat burning effect. So fast can also mean fat burning! Clearly this type of workout couldn't be maintained for extensive periods but overall, it highlights that whilst all exercise is beneficial for health and fitness, there are additional benefits to be gained from periodically pushing your boundaries.

So to help you get greater benefits from your workouts, here are the top five ways to maximise your calorie burn when you exercise.

How to burn more fat during your workout

- **Run to the hills!** Running is a great calorie burner, in fact it is burns the most calories of any cardiovascular exercise and similar to your car, the faster you go, the more fuel you burn. However, if you really want to rev up the calorie burning effect then head for the hills. When you climb hills you use a lot more energy to 'drag' your bodyweight uphill so a really effective session is to transplant your usual route onto a hilly course, working hard up the hills. Not only will you burn more calories but you'll also improve your leg strength and give your CV system a better quality workout as well!

- **Weight for it!** Lifting weights is also a great calorie burner, something that many people are unaware of. People are often surprised to discover the all-round results that they achieve from incorporating resistance exercises into their training because the great benefit of toning up and building some muscle is the extra calorie burning benefits that you get from your workout extends after your workout – in fact permanently! The energy cost to your body of supporting lean muscle is greater than body-fat and hence if you tone up, you enhance your calorie burn all the time.

- **Boost your weights workouts.** If you really want to enhance your fat burning during a resistance training session, intersperse some weight-training exercises with some CV exercise! Instead of taking recovery periods between weight exercises, jump onto a piece of CV equipment for a fast 5 minute burst. Vary the equipment each time, from the treadmill to the rower, bike and cross-trainer so you exercise different muscle groups and you'll find that you really give your metabolic rate a boost both from the weight-training and the CV workouts. Additionally, you'll find that you can cram a lot more into your standard session which means you'll get fitter as well!

- **Choose your class with care . . .** If you prefer group exercise classes to other forms of exercise then to maximise your fat burning you need to make sure that you get the most out of your time in the class. Doing the same class regularly can get you in a rut unless you continually focus on the quality of your session. If you enjoy a circuit-type class, re-challenge your body by selecting some different weights or if you prefer aerobics, avoid coasting during parts of the workout – focus on maintaining the intensity all the time – so that you get better value from your exercise time and get those calorie burning benefits!

- **Be a good sport.** Of course, some people simply enjoy a specific sport as their way of keeping fit and their weight in check. Think about how you play your sport. Do you always play in the same position? Do you favour doubles over singles? A small change can make a big difference so for example playing tennis singles instead of doubles will increase your workload and intensity and burn more calories and rotating a defender up to midfield or attack will often result in more running – and a greater fat burn.

YOUR Time

> *'The bird of time has not far to fly and the bird is on the wing!'*
>
> ***ANON***

It's time for YOU!

'I'd like to be fitter but I'm just too busy to exercise' – is a very common statement and also an unsurprising one given the modern day pressures that we currently live under. Work, stress, family commitments (to name just three), frequently mean that you end up burning the candle at both ends trying to fit everything in. Of course in achieving that, something has to slip and invariably that is time for YOU! Time for you is time where you can switch off from all those commitments and focus on important things in your life and there can be few more important things than maintaining your health and fitness – long-term. Exercise is so effective at combating the effects of a stressful lifestyle – for example after a good workout, away from the demands of the mobile phone and inbox, you look more relaxed, feel more relaxed and have made a major contribution to improving and maintaining your health.

Time for your exercise does need a little planning though but once you've built it into your routine and felt the benefits that it brings, you'll wonder how you ever managed without it! To help you create some time for you, follow these time-saving exercise tips and start feeling the benefits!

Super 8 time-saving exercise tips

1. **Just say no!** Easier said than done but saying no to requests from people to complete tasks that aren't your responsibility will help free up spare time – for you.

2. **Keep that kitbag.** If you haven't got your gear with you, when the opportunity arises, you won't be able to exercise. A cancelled appointment, a business trip, or even when you're on holiday; are all opportunities to manage a workout. Simply pack a sports bag with your usual exercise kit so that when you get the chance, you can enjoy a training session.

3. **Make an appointment – with yourself!** It might sound bizarre but booking a slot in your diary for YOUR time makes sense and will help you to factor exercise into your day.

4. **Alternate your exercises.** If you enjoy working out with weights, instead of taking rests between sets, carry out an alternative exercise during you rest period. For example, do a chest exercise followed by an upper back exercise and then repeat. This way you can cut your exercise time by up to 50% and get a more challenging workout.

5. **Ramp up the intensity.** One way to get more from your CV workout in less time is to vary the intensity of your run, walk, jog, swim etc. Instead of completing your sessions at the same pace, spice it up a little by injecting some faster paced bursts. You will challenge your body more – but equally you can get fitter with fewer workouts. It is important to remember though that your exercise sessions should always be carefully structured around your personal fitness levels and personal goals for safety and injury free progression.

6. **Ask the family!** Share and share alike – and that means the chores too! Get all your family involved in helping with everyday tasks so that it's not always left just for you. If everyone chips in, tasks can be completed faster and most importantly, there'll be more time for you to get fitter.

7. **Combine your workouts.** No time to get to the gym? Too busy for an early evening jog? Try combining exercise with your commute to work or other weekly tasks. Cycling and walking are both great cardiovascular exercise and with a little ingenuity, can often be combined with the school run, commute or a local shopping trip.

8. **Stay indoors!** If the worst comes to the worst, you can still take beneficial exercise without leaving the comfort of your own home. Flexibility training is a vital component of a balanced exercise programme and is easy to do in your own lounge. Core exercises and a workout with dumbbells can also be completed in a very small space if necessary, so by shifting the coffee table you can convert your front room into a mini gym!

You can fit fitness into your life!

Completing five cardiovascular (CV), two resistance training and two flexibility training sessions each week is impossible to fit in – isn't it? To fit all that exercise into a week you'd have to live at the gym and spend countless hours churning out road miles – and that's not even considering your flexibility training – wouldn't you? Well, breathe easily because you don't need to commit to such a huge volume of training – if you train smartly. Everyone is pushed for time these days as we attempt to cram more and more into each successive 24 hours but the solution is to exercise smartly, incorporating exercise into your life as opposed to letting it dominate your life. By maximising your training benefits each session, you can get fit, achieve genuine fitness gains and stay fit – long-term.

So why try the total body fitness challenge that gives you a CV, flexibility and total body workout – and all for approximately 4 hours per week . . !

All-round fitness for 4 hours per week

- **Commit.** To begin with you need to commit to your training. This programme brings results but only if you are prepared to maximise your training time during each session. So that means combination workouts, fewer rest periods and focusing upon quality throughout. However, the upside of your commitment is that you will find that you can fit fitness into your life and after all, 4 hours is less than 3% of your weekly time.

- **CV sessions**. Your target is 3 sessions per week or their equivalent.
    - **At the weekend:** One extended workout building up to 60 minutes of non-stop CV exercise. This will build your endurance and counts as two CV sessions. *Training time = 1 hour.*

    - **During the week:** One combination CV and resistance training session (see details below) and two general activity CV sessions which you can combine with other activities. For example these sessions could comprise a bike ride or a walk into or from work which means that you don't need to factor in extra exercise time. If you do find that you've got some spare time then of course you can go to the gym or do a separate session but this programme is all about fitting exercise into your life when you're busy, so combination CV sessions can really help. *Training time = 2 hours.*

- **Resistance training sessions.** Target 2 sessions per week.
    - **Session 1.** This is a dedicated weights session, comprising a warm-up, followed by a two sets of a range of exercises that specifically target all the primary muscle groups around the body, followed by a cool down and some stretching. *Training time = 1 hour.*
    - **Session 2.** A combination CV and resistance training session comprising a total body resistance training workout, with a single set of repetitions for each exercise, interspersed with short 5 minute bursts of CV exercise, which gives you with CV and strength training all within the one session! Training time = 1 hour but note that this hour has already been accounted for in your CV training above!

- **Flexibility training:** Your target is a minimum of 2 sessions per week. However, flexibility training doesn't significantly eat into your time because you're typically holding each stretch for approximately 30 seconds. Hence, as part of your cool down after each session, allot 5 minutes for stretching the primary muscles that you've worked.

  Eg: After a CV session, focus on leg stretches for 5 minutes and after a weights workout, target upper body flexibility exercises. The beauty of tackling your flexibility training in this way is that you're already warmed up so you're body is ideally prepared for a stretching session and by combining it within your other workouts, it incurs no additional training time! *Training time = nil.*

- **Putting it all together.** So, now the training's been broken down, how do you fit it all together?
    - 1 x weekend based extended CV session (counting as 2 CV sessions) + flexibility = 1 hour.
    - 2 x general activity CV sessions (counting as 2 CV sessions) = 1 hour.
    - 1 x dedicated resistance training + flexibility session = 1 hour
    - 1 x combination CV and resistance training session + flexibility = 1 hour

So, now you genuinely can follow a fitness programme that you can blend into your home, work and social life without it taking over your life.

and finally . . .

Sometimes, getting your health and fitness on track can seem just too big a nut to crack. There's too much to learn, too much to do, too much to organise, too much to fit in and too little time in which to achieve it; which is understandable given the pressures of *'21st century syndrome'*.

Think about this then. Cast your mind back to the last time you were ill. Not ill with a mild cold but properly ill in bed – perhaps with proper flu and unable to do anything. How did that feel? What was your focus? What did you crave? At those unfortunate times in your life, your focus was total. Only one thing mattered. Material possessions, climbing the corporate ladder, chasing the £, daily trivia; they all paled into insignificance because you only sought one goal.

And that single goal was to get better and to feel good. Most ill health isn't down to disease or bad luck, it's down to misuse. Remember, you only get given one body – it's got to last you all your life . . .

www.body4life.co.uk